"A terrific way to assess whether your current situation is what you really want."
Steven King, Founder and Chairman,
Hotel Discovery Restaurants

"This made me stop and think about a lot of things... especially whether my actions are consistent with my words."
Larry Olson, President
Natural Golf Corporation

"The chapter on coping with conflict and stress is a real jewel. I want all of our key people to have a copy."
Tom Heimsoth, Chairman,
Resource Information Management Systems

"Excellent tool for core training."
Kathryn W. Ling, President,
The Leadership Edge

"Every chapter contains vital information for everyone who wants to be self-motivated."
Joseph A. Piscopo, Founder
Pansophic Systems

D0111189

OTHER BOOKS BY ROGER FRITZ

One Step Ahead

The Unused
Keys to Success

Roger Fritz

Sage
Creek
Press

TRAVERSE CITY, MICHIGAN

Published by *Sage Creek Press*
121 E. Front Street, 4th Floor
Traverse City, Michigan 49684

Publisher's Cataloging-in-Publication Data
Fritz, Roger.
   One step ahead: the unused keys tol success /
   Roger Fritz. – Traverse City, MI: Sage Creek Press, 1998.
      p.   ill   cm.
   Includes bibliographical references and index.
   ISBN 1-890394-19-X
   1.Success in business. 2. Success. 3. Interpersonal relations. I. Title.
HF5386.F75   1998   98-84654
650.1'3   dc—21   CIP

PROJECT COORDINATION BY JENKINS GROUP, INC.

02 01 00 99   ♦   5 4 3 2 1

Printed in the United States of America

For Nanc and Sue
who are always one step ahead.

Contents

❖ Contents ❖

Preface

THIS BOOK HAS A VERY SIMPLE PURPOSE: TO HELP YOU identify and build on those critical areas that are essential for achieving the success you want at work and in your personal relationships. In other words—to help you create your own success! Keep in mind, however, that success is personal...it means what it means to you.

In a very real sense, this book is incomplete because it requires your unique input and contribution. It has been prepared, not to do something for you, but to provide a focus and format to work *with* you.

As you become involved with the processes written here, some special benefits can be achieved. You can:

- Focus attention on selecting specific goals that are essential to your unique definition of success.

- Eliminate activities that are not essential.

- Determine the step-by-step process needed to change yourself first before you try to change other people.

- Create the climate necessary for others to deal more effectively with you at work.

- Evaluate the results you are achieving, and how to use them as a springboard to even greater accomplishment.

- Match yourself with a job that enables you to capitalize on your unique abilities.

- Begin to plan and plot the best routes to attain your unrealized potential-a lifelong process!

When all is said and done
your value to others depends on only
*one thing—**how much they need you!***

Chapter 1

THE UNUSED KEYS TO SUCCESS

How Successful People Prepare Themselves

S OMETIME DURING THEIR LIVES, MOST PEOPLE ARE LIKELY to reflect on the accomplishments they have achieved. For some, their success can be calculated in terms of personal power. For others, it's the accumulation of great wealth. A few bask in the light of instant recognition. Notoriety, for a relative few, is sufficient indication of having "made it."

Yet, other men and women view success on a totally different scale. They measure it by the length of constructive contributions made to the society in which they live.

Regardless of the yardstick used, success comes to

those who are willing to enlarge their abilities, store their minds with useful information, and have the desire and drive to reach specific objectives.

Consider two cases from today's headlines:

Bill Gates, founder and chairman of Microsoft Corporation, is the richest man in the world. His personal fortune is approaching $40 billion.

A complex man, he is a rare mixture of genius and generosity. Fiercely competitive as a businessman, he was extremely introverted and shy as a boy.

Close friends say he never feels uneasy among brilliant people, but has little patience with stupidity.

His challenge to Microsoft managers is to hire people who quickly adapt to changing conditions and find solutions to new problems.

His dominance in the hi-tech sector has brought many critics and even powerful enemies. Having found un-used keys to success in the business world, he is already thinking about his life after Microsoft and is committed to giving away 95 percent of his wealth. If his choices and decisions in that role are as good as they have been until now, every human being in the world will benefit.

Isiah Thomas was, until recently, the highest-ranking African American in professional sports as the general manager of the Toronto Raptors in the National Basketball Association. But, you have to know his mother to understand how he became unstoppable. Born in poverty, the youngest of nine children, his father left when he was three. Friends have vivid memories of his mother with a gun on the front porch saying, "Any of you come around with drugs, this is what you get!" And she meant it!

Isiah's philosophy is simple, but powerful. "My goal," he says, "is to work, to prepare and to leave no stone unturned." Asked to identify the changes needed in his profession, he doesn't hesitate to answer. "A lot of problems come from player security. There's no incentive for a player to work. It's as if they think they don't need to get any better."[1]

Easy to see why, isn't it? That's the exact opposite of how he became unstoppable.

What is Success?

Some people's definitions of success are as selfish as they are bleak. To them, success means projecting the proper image. Being well-dressed is all-important. Being seen with the right people in the right places means that they have truly arrived. To others, the pressure to excel is so intense that the thought they may have to crawl over the bodies of friends or co-workers doesn't faze them in the least. In fact, they are willing to sacrifice what it is they *really* want, to bring success within their grasp. Consequences? They'll worry about

---

1. *American Way*, November 1997

them later. For now they're content to watch for signs that lead to the kinds of success they crave.

Others take a more mature view of success. They seek out their best qualities and refine or bring them to fruition. Their ambition is to contribute something constructive to the human experience. Their idea of success is helping the community in which they live achieve a worthwhile goal. Working with the needy. Contributing to a project at work that will streamline an operation, enhance profits, provide openings for new hires, or overcome an obstacle to progress. They are willing to pay their way in the human scene.

One need not look long to find inspiring examples.

Mother Teresa had few of the worldly possessions most people think essential to the good life. Yet her days were filled with personal satisfaction and accomplishment, working among India's poorest and dispossessed people.

Not long ago, the president of a major corporation resigned his $1-million-a-year salary to work full-time as a volunteer leader for several charities with whom he has been associated. Why? Because he had prepared others who were now well-qualified to do what he'd been doing. Besides, he felt a completely different kind of satisfaction after making the change.

Or, take the case of the middle-aged bachelor in Illinois who won $2.3 million in the state lottery. He lived alone in a small apartment, drove a ten-year-old car, and felt he was already successful. He reasoned that he made $520 a week, which was enough for him. He liked his work and the way he lived. His special pleasure is watching sports on television. He wondered what he could possibly do with so much money. His decision? He gave it all to a young couple with two children who had befriended him.

Daniel Huffman is an eighteen-year-old high school senior. A football star, his dream was to play at a major university and then become a pro. But, he gave it up so his grandmother could live...he gave her a kidney.

Raised by his father and grandparents, he drove his grandmother to dialysis treatment three times a week for two years. As she continued to fail, he talked to nurses and surgeons—then made his decision-he would not risk waiting for a kidney donor.

His explanation is a powerful definition of how to become unstoppable. "I love my grandmother," he says, "but it was just as much for me as it was for her, because I didn't want to lose her."

Another interesting aspect of success is that you can become trapped by it. That is, in your effort to hold on to fame and notoriety, you must exceed previous successes until the chase becomes all-consuming. Then a tendency to believe that failure is intolerable may develop, when actually, failure can be helpful because it lets us know when we're off the track.

Interesting examples would include Howard

Hughes, Elvis Presley, Marilyn Monroe, John Belushi, and Chris Farley—five successful people, richer than most of us ever dream of becoming, whose personal lives were a mess. Four died as a result of drugs, the fifth (Hughes) alone and utterly abandoned. Each was exploited by others. How does one measure their success?

If we equate success with happiness, then it seems obvious that neither is directly related to the accumulation of possessions. **Success is an attitude.**

> **We are successful when we genuinely appreciate what we have and do not allow ourselves to be depressed because of what we don't have.**

Success Essentials

Put simply, motivation is the urge to succeed, whether in serving on a committee or seeking position and power in a multi-national corporation. It may be the drive to achieve success in business, serve mankind in one of the professions, or add something to the beauty of life through one of the arts.

The key to success is in working persistently toward specific objectives under your own power. You must assume that you can count on nobody but yourself. More than that, success means progressing from what is acceptable to what is excellent. This suggests that success seldom comes easy; getting things done is, more often than not, the result of a long, tough apprenticeship. Seven personal attributes are essential to achieving success potential:

1. **Self-Esteem.** Unless you regard yourself as a valuable individual-a worthy and capable human being-there's little chance you'll be able to change or control the conditions and opportunities that lead to success.

2. **Responsibility.** Another word for guts. You hold yourself strictly accountable for what happens in your life. You willingly assume full responsibility for the events that result in either success or failure.

3. **Optimism.** Those who are successful understand clearly that there are situations beyond the scope of their capabilities, but they do not lose their sense of proportion. They feel good about themselves, have confidence in the future, and work productively in the present.

4. **Goals.** Success is measured step by step. One must know how far he or she has come toward achieving one's goals. Success-oriented individuals keep their goals before them constantly. Not only do goals measure progress, but they also serve to motivate and direct behavior.

5. **Imagination.** Those without imagination can't visualize what it might be like to experience excit-

ing, new, and beneficial ventures before they occur. Successful people use their imaginations constantly and creatively, testing ideas in the light of possibilities.

6. **Awareness.** The alert succeed because they are aware of the world around them. They know what's going on, who is doing what, and when. More importantly, their eyes are open to new opportunities.

7. **Creativity.** The successful make a habit of looking at problems, situations, and even opportunities, from a number of different vantage points. They question constantly: Why is this so? What makes it different? When did it happen? Who will benefit most from change or a new direction? What would happen if...?

Another quality, one so obvious it is often overlooked, is the ability to listen for the knock that announces opportunity. Too many people sit back and wait patiently for fortune to smile on them. In a surprising number of instances, when fortune finally does knock, it is unheard; when it smiles broadly, it is ignored. The ability to recognize the "lucky" break is a vital skill because it doesn't happen often.

Take Adolph Zukor, a Hungarian immigrant, as an example. Coming to this country at the turn of the century, Zukor, who was later to become head of

Paramount Studios, took over a nickelodeon as partial payment for a debt. It didn't take him long to recognize that here was a genuine opportunity for making a fortune just waiting to be seized. The nickelodeon was new and novel; it had great possibilities for expansion. It also had some king-size problems that inhibited its development.

- Animation on film ranged from dull to monotonous. (Where's the excitement or love interest in watching the Niagara River fall?

- Because films were short, only about five minutes in length, the amount of money that could be asked of patrons was limited-about a penny a minute. A slow way to make a fortune.

- Downtime was frequent. Film continually slipped from the reel, causing delays and frustration to both the operator and viewers.

But what if the film was longer? Would it be possible to film an entire play—even an opera? Isn't it likely people would willingly pay more to see such spectacales?

Zukor explained the problems as he saw them to the nickelodeon's inventor, Thomas A. Edison. Edison quickly recognized the opportunities, too. But, in order to increase the length of films, reels would have to be bigger, and some way would have to be found to keep the film from slipping off. If a longer film could be held in place on a larger reel, then the potential was limit-less.

Suddenly a light dawned. Suppose the reels had teeth that held the film in place. Sprocket holes! That was the answer. Edison quickly punched a series of holes on both sides of a film strip, and the modern movie business was born.

Less dramatic perhaps, but equally opportunistic, is the realization of the dream two young women from Georgia had when they converted their at-home hobby into a $5 million-a-year business. Together they began to manufacture women's and children's sportswear. Today, their apparel line is distributed nationwide by more than two dozen sales reps.

They began their business almost by accident. Because the local school library needed funds, the partners decided to create garments to help raise the money. What they produced was such a terrific hit, they decided to sell some items on their own for profit. Later, they displayed their finest creations at Atlanta's Apparel Mart. It was then that they took the plunge into a serious business.

A major obstacle to their growth has been limited production. Most of their garments are made by hand, one at a time by other homemakers who make the items during the hours their youngsters are in school. Realizing that success depended not only on top qual-ity but speed as well, the partners invested in a multi-head embroidering machine that can produce six to twelve garments simultaneously.

What is the essential ingredient responsible for this company's success? It can be summed up in six short words: the owners like what they do.

Success Factors

Successful people also have a knack for remaining cool under fire. They demonstrate their emotional maturity and stability best when the going gets rough. While others are bumbling about in confusion, these steadfast individuals will never lose sight of the goals they feel are important to achieve. They're simply too absorbed in doing what is necessary to worry much about obstacles or momentary delays.

The same holds true for making decisions. The timid make certain no mistakes will ever be chalked up to them by simply ducking decisions. It has been said that ninety percent of the world's failure are quitters.

This is likely what Charles F. Kettering, one of the founders of General Motors, had in mind when he observed that, "No one would ever cross the ocean if he could get off the ship in a storm."

Avoiding Failure is Not the Same as Achieving Success

Successful people maintain a realistic view of what is possible for others to achieve. If they are in positions of leadership, which is often the case, they're savvy enough not to set standards so high that they are beyond the capacity of others to meet. At the same time, however, standards they do set cause those they lead to reach. In the process, they are often pleasantly surprised by what they are actually able to accomplish.

Typical of the gumption to move ahead without much reassurance or support is the case of the electric light. Pooh-poohed by all the experts, the idea seemed doomed until a thirty-one-year-old American inventor, Thomas A. Edison, announced he was working on an incandescent lamp. The British Parliament decided to check out the invention and even set up a committee to investigate his progress.

The committee's conclusions are interesting. The distinguished witnesses reported (to the great relief of all gas companies) that Edison's ideas were "good enough for our transatlantic friends, but unworthy of the attention of practical or scientific men." How about that for foresight?

A case in point is Lee Iacocca, who is credited with resurrecting Chrysler Corporation from bankruptcy. In a razor-edged interview with Bonnie Remsberg for *Success Magazine*, Iacocca talked about the qualities he seeks in people with whom he worked:

> "The kind of people I look for to fill top management spots are the eager beavers, the mavericks. These are the guys who try to do more than they're expected to

do—they always reach. They're always interfacing with the people they work with, trying to help them do their jobs better. That's the way they're built.

There are other guys, the ones in the 9 to 5 group. They just want to get along and be told what to do. They say, I don't want to be in the rat race, it might affect my heartbeat.

Listen, just because you get involved and get excited and really tear into things doesn't mean you're in a rat race or that you'll die of hypertension next week! I mean people read too much about that stuff.

When I interview a guy for a job, I'm real good with first impressions. I get a feel about him. I can tell whether he's any good at this work or not. But I can't tell whether he's savvy, meaning he's got common sense, until I've been with him a few months. Another thing I can't tell is whether he's got that vision, that drive, that spark, or is he really built lazy.

You find a guy who's a Phi Beta Kappa. He's had experience and he looks terrific. He's articulate, makes a good speech. And then you find out he's lazy. There's nothing you can do about it.

So you try to look for people with that drive. You don't need many. I could run the United States with 25 guys. I don't think you need 100.

I can run Chrysler with a dozen goodies-'horses,' I call 'em. They do most of the work anyway, they really do. The reason they're horses is they know how to delegate and motivate. They know how to look for pressure points and set priorities. They say, "forget that; it'll take ten years. Here's what we gotta do now."

If you pick a guy for a key slot and find out you've made a mistake, you get rid of him. In my years at Chrysler I brought in a lot of new people. In this kind of situation you might get one who turns out to be a complete, utter dud. If you do, you have to get rid of him. We have a few maybe who aren't living up to expectations, but they're not in critical jobs. If they're in critical jobs, you have to dump them. That's ruthless, but it has to be done.

The worst thing you can do for an organization is live with a mistake like that. Before you know it, all the secretaries know he's a dud and they think the boss doesn't know it because he's not doing anything about it.

We've been fortunate in the people we've had at Chrysler. We retired a lot of people because they were of another era—the age of the Golden Goose, when you sold cars and made tons of money even though you were inefficient or mediocre—and if they couldn't change their habits, they got booted out.

Not because I thought it was a pleasant way to run things, but what are you going to do?

I guess if I had to say only one thing about management, it would be that the key is decisiveness.

You can use computers and gather all the facts in the world, but in the end you have to get them together, set a timetable, and *act*.

I know people who wait to have 100 percent of the facts in, with research that guarantees a program is going to work. They want to be certain because they are going to be spending $100 million. But by the time they get all that put together, their decision isn't timely. It may be right, but it's too late, and they got clobbered in the marketplace.

Now you need the facts. If you move with only 50 percent of the facts, then you're flying by the seat of your pants and you'd better be lucky or have good hunches. You can't run companies that way. But you must make timely decisions.

In our business, it's murder. It's changing all the time, and you have to guess what's going to appeal three years down the road. We have new models, but how do I know what's going to sell tomorrow?"[2]

In interviews, during discussions—even in television commercials for his company—Lee Iacocca reflected a toughness of purpose and a driving determination to win. He's a "let's tell it like it is and get on

2. Reprinted with permission of the author, Bonnie Remsberg from *Success*, January 1982.

with it" type of executive. Are these the same qualities he seeks in the men and women who are destined to fill top posts at Chrysler? You bet it is. Those who turn out best in Iacocca's candid and often colorful opinion could be described as follows:

- *Risk-Taking Mavericks*—The cool, calculating chance-takers with enough guts to lay their jobs on the line if necessary, to get a new, untested but important project underway.

- *Controlled Workaholics*—The eight-hour day for these people is the exception rather than the routine. They find their jobs so exciting and challenging that actual time at work holds little interest or meaning for them. What does count is accomplishment. That's the kind of compensation that seems to satisfy them best.

- *Honest Communicators*—They speak out bravely, even at the risk of being blunt. What they believe can be achieved is stated in a way that stimulates their listeners to action. More than that, they create a climate in which two-way communication is encouraged. The ideas they express are clear and adequate. Factual feedback follows as a natural course of events.

- *Fearless Delegators*—They have no fear of delegating important tasks to others. Employees get the chance to succeed or fail on their own. They motivate their people by example so they're encouraged to do their best.

- *Practical Planners*—They have the foresight to see the task in total, rather than attempting to handle important jobs in bits and pieces. They force themselves to think ahead, set priorities and measure progress as accurately as possible.

- *Tough-Minded Deciders*—If it means dropping a favorite but no longer valuable program, they don't hesitate. If a veteran employee is no longer effective—after a fair chance—then he or she must be replaced, however personally painful the departure may be.

- *Dreamers With Horse Sense*—They'll tolerate the dreamer as long as the dream has a chance of working. But, they also look for concrete results within a reasonable time—not sometime in the distant future. Priority is the measure used—not expectations. They know how to use facts to reach timely decisions, even though their business is in a constant state of flux.

- *Sacrificial Performers*—They willingly do more than is reasonably expected of them—not because they're apple polishers, but because that's how they're built. When they get excited, they generate excitement in others. Working with others is a joy, never a chore. They cooperate.

They interact. But if they must go it alone, they don't pout. While they have tremendous energy output, it's directed and controlled. Most important of all, they have sufficient emotional backbone to keep going—despite a lack of encouragement-once they know they're on the right track.

As Lee Iacocca suggests, success depends on how well we communicate. To be successful, one must know the importance of creating a climate in which two-way communication is possible. Successful communicators express ideas clearly. Equally important, they make certain there's adequate factual feedback. Mr. Iacocca would seem to play that role to perfection.

> **Ultimately, success depends on the ability to sustain effort even without deserved praise. It is true that as responsibilities increase, recognition often decreases. Therefore, those who want success must have the emotional backbone to keep going, even without reassurance and support.**

The key is the ability to look inward for an evaluation of personal strengths and abilities-to realize that praise from others isn't really that important.

Do You Know Yourself?

Not sure? Then maybe an introduction is in order. The Success Factor Evaluation Form (Figure1.1) can help you get acquainted with the most important person you'll ever know. It will help you get to know the real you. Here's what to do:

- Review each of the five major headings on the chart.

- Think about your recent decisions involving emotional maturity, timely decisions, patience/tolerance capabilities, communications, and lack of recognition.

- Jot down the situation as briefly as possible, but be sure to include the key factors.

- Note what happened as a result of your actions or activities.

- Indicate how you might now handle the situation.

Figure 1.1 provides some interesting insights into your potential for success. Certainly, it should help you answer the questions in Figure 1.2 objectively.

If your answers to these questions (and others likely to come to mind) have been objective, then any fantasies about yourself should quickly dissolve. In their place, a clear picture of your potential for success will emerge.

The most intense need of any person is to determine the strength of their ambition, and the full extent of their abilities. An awareness of weakness is as vital as the identification of strength. Only in this way is it possible to work toward overcoming weaknesses, and capitalizing on strengths.

FIGURE 1.1
SUCCESS FACTOR EVALUATION FORM

Emotional Maturity

Recent Emotional Decision	Objective/Goal	Result?

Timely Decisions

Recent Delayed Decisions	Mistake Feared	Why?

Patience/Tolerance Expectation

Recent Example of Standards *Too High* for Others	Result?

FIGURE 1.1 (continued)

Recent Example of Standards *Too Low* for Others	Result?

Communications

Most Serious Grievances Against You	Action Plan?
Your Most Serious Grievances	Action Plan?

Lack of Recognition

My Substitutes for Praise Are:	Effectiveness?	If Not, Which Might Be?

Figure 1.2
My Success Potential

Am I goal oriented? Am I dedicated to reaching the goals I've established?	( )Yes	( )No
Do I demonstrate a high degree of self-reliance? Or, in times of stress or crisis, do I tend to lean on others for support?	( )Yes	( )No
Do I utilize a creative approach in reaching decisions or solutions to problems?	( )Yes	( )No
Or, do I make use of a "formula" with which I feel comfortable?	( )Yes	( )No
Do I make full use of my imagination as well as my intelligence?	( )Yes	( )No
Do people usually trust decisions I want to implement?	( )Yes	( )No
Do they willingly assist in implementing my decisions?	( )Yes	( )No
Are the standards I set for myself usually higher than those I establish for friends, family, or employees?	( )Yes	( )No
Do I sometimes hear via the grapevine that the standards I establish for others are out of reach?	( )Yes	( )No
Or, ridiculously easy?	( )Yes	( )No
Do people with whom I frequently communicate usually react positively to suggestions or proposals I offer?	( )Yes	( )No
Do I come across clearly to others?	( )Yes	( )No
Do I make an earnest effort to stimulate feedback from others?	( )Yes	( )No
Am I able to shrug off what appears to be a lack of appreciation from superiors for work well done?	( )Yes	( )No
Am I still able to continue doing a creditable job even when there is no thank you?	( )Yes	( )No
Do I demonstrate courage by standing behind those who must carry out a decision I have made?	( )Yes	( )No
Am I optimistic most of the time? When I'm down do I bounce back rapidly?	( )Yes	( )No
Do I feel that I am in good health?	( )Yes	( )No

Tips on Seizing Success

Without question, a major stride taken on the road to success is the development of self-confidence. Everyone does something well. Concentrate on your forte. Pinpoint the skills and talents that can become the backbone of your success.

Next, focus your energies. This doesn't mean necessarily putting in extra hours on the job or working weekends—although that sometimes may be necessary. It *does* mean developing a driving determination to get things done. One practical way to concentrate your energies is simply to split your days up into manageable time segments. Not only do you acquire an exhilarating feeling of accomplishment when a good job is turned in on schedule, but you also fuel your energies, so they're red hot and ready to take on the next important task.

> **Failure is determined in large part by what we allow to happen—success by what we make happen.**

Certainly initiative to assume full responsibility is an important key to success. You must be willing to accept responsibility for any tasks assigned to you, or goals you're directed to achieve—even the actions of those with whom you work. The same holds true for achieving success at home or in school. Seek out responsibility if it isn't offered. Take on the chores everyone else is unwilling to assume—or has successfully ducked.

Develop a sense of what works in your organization to get ahead; a *house style*, if you like. If your company favors the tough-talking competitive type—or demands a ruthless twenty-four-hours-a-day dedication to the bottom line—go for it. The same advice holds true for dress and deportment, as well as life off the job.

Don't wait to be told. Observe. Ask questions. Listen to others and link their ambitions to your goals. Take action and deliver on your promises.

Keep your cool. Your personal emotions should play no role in reaching tough, analytical decisions. Before you blow your top in public, talk it out with yourself—in private. Reduce anxieties by acting out the situation—alone. Ask yourself "What's the worst that can happen?" Then, let your answer guide your actions. Another benefit: you avoid the tendency to run others down, or place blame irresponsibly.

None of this happens by chance, of course. The self-directed individual knows that a negative approach to any situation automatically puts the brakes on progress. To substantially reduce such a possibility, workable guidelines have to be established. This means scanning the territory for yourself. Observe what is going on. Make your own appraisal. Set up a personal plan of action.

To summarize, research has revealed that those who soar to success in business, as well as in other fields, possess certain characteristics in common. They have, for instance:

- **Strong, outgoing personalities.** They appear self-confident and self-sufficient. Their drive is powerful and self-sustaining.

- **A knack for appearing unflappable.** Because they've developed skill at analyzing and defining situations precisely, they remain calm, even in the face of embarrassing or challenging situations.

- **Energy to spare.** Their vitality is explosive—even when engaged in sports or other leisure-time activities.

- **Self-assurance.** While there is never a question about what they feel must be done, they're not so assertive that it turns others off. Though they have an ability to command attention, they do so pleasantly. They behave considerately toward others.

- **Daring.** The unfamiliar holds few terrors for them. They adapt easily and quickly. Perhaps this is one of the reasons why employees stand loyally by them and willingly carry out instructions at any time.

It might seem wonderful if someone laid out patterns of thought and action for us. But then success would not only be impossible, there would be no personal satisfaction in having stood on one's own feet, or appreciation of going it alone to reach a desirable destination.

Developing Your Success Plan

> The side roads are filled with brainy people who started fast but ran out of gas. They were replaced by slower, plain, deliberate types who just kept going and never looked back.

Knowing just how far you've traveled on the road to success is vital. An effective way to pinpoint your exact location is to answer these questions:

- What are my major strengths? (Excellent planner, strong work ethic, get along well with others, etc.)

- What weaknesses have I identified that may inhibit my progress? (Poor communicator, won't delegate, fail to give credit to others, impatient, lack of schooling, etc.)

- What have been my major achievements? In the past thirty days? Last quarter? Six months? Year?

- How did these achievements relate to my accountability?

- Did I achieve the priorities identified as vital? If not, why?

- What did I learn in the past twelve months that will help me succeed in the future?

- What important objectives for which I was responsible were achieved?

- What important objectives did I fail to achieve? Why?

- Who, other than myself, contributed significantly to the accomplishment of these objectives?

- What outside factors influenced my success or failure?

Once you understand precisely where you are, it is then possible to establish one or more realistic, specific, achievable objectives—based on facts you have learned about yourself and the environment in which you must work or live. To move in the direction essential for your success, your objectives must meet the following three criteria:

1. They Must Be *Realistic.* Can they be achieved within a reasonable length of time? What costs are involved? Will they bring about desired changes?

2. They Must Be *Specific.* Do they specify when results can be expected? Do they say what benefits or improvements will be achieved? Do they state what results are sought?

3. They Must Ensure *Improvement.* Do they offer sufficient challenge? Will they overcome problems, seize opportunities? Do they offer the chance to be of service to others?

When you have decided on a destination, the next step is to select routes that will take you there. Speed at this point isn't everything: being prepared has a fit and proper place in programming your plan. Your most important concern is making certain you're on the right road and that you're ready for the journey.

Here are some tips to help you do just that. Base your program for improvement on these components:

- The objectives you've established.

- A written, step-by-step outline of actions you plan to take (return to school, volunteer services to a local organization, gaining additional experience on the job, etc.).

- A time limit.

- An estimate of costs (dollars, time off the job, etc.).

- A determination of support required (from a supervisor, spouse, friends, source materials, etc.).

As you can see, the program phase of a success plan is the action step. Not only does it provide a clear-cut route to your objectives, but it also helps to minimize chances for error or the possibility of overlooking an essential detail.

To keep your success plan on course, it's important to check frequently for change, deviations, or new opportunities that may require immediate attention.

How do you know when it's time to make a switch in

a job or in a career? Tip-offs used by a success-oriented man and woman can provide some solid clues.

The woman now owns two prosperous travel agencies, as well as several other enterprises closely allied with the travel industry. When her career plan was detoured by a boss who refused her a promotion because she was a woman, she played it cool and took stock of the situation. Careful analysis suggested some wide-open opportunities nearby for knowledgeable travel agents. Once the decision was made, she walked.

The man grew increasingly frustrated when he did not receive so much as a thank you for ideas that kept his company's profit and loss statement in the black. He told friends that he simply got tired of turning his brain over to someone else for a paycheck. After looking around, he saw an opportunity in software development and proceeded to build a highly profitable business in that field.

Obviously, if your program is working well and objectives are being achieved on schedule, then you will want to leave well enough alone. But to make certain there are no slip-ups or oversights, use the checkpoints below as a guide. Begin by asking yourself:

- Is my success plan on target? Am I on schedule? What events seem to upset my timetable? Are there new activities, problems, or responsibilities interfering with what I have to achieve? What are they?

- What additional effort or assistance my be required? Who can I turn to for assistance? What sources should I check? How much additional time may be required?

- What adjustments to my plan or program may be necessary?

- Do I see specific results? Changes in the attitude of others toward me? Increased returns on time invested? Tangible successes? Greater motivation to help others? More fun on the job and in activities with others? Excitement over new challenges? Growing confidence in myself? Cooperation where none existed before?

Take Action Now

We hear a lot these days about the need for a strategy—for a company—for a job—for a career. My concern is that we may make the definition too complicated. The essential idea is that we (1) think seriously about the future and (2) learn to ask tough questions in attempting to anticipate everything we can. The first step is to answer the "What if" questions, which will eliminate unpleasant surprises. For example:

- What if the approach we agreed upon bogs down?

- What if Plan A costs more than we budgeted?

- What if new competition appears after we commit for expansion?

- What if current competition under-prices us in the second quarter?

- What if my confidence in my new boss isn't justified?

- What if my trusted staff fails to perform as expected?

- What if my graduate degree doesn't impress my new employer?

- What if my health problem worsens and I can't keep my present work pace?

- What if I'm asked to transfer to a job I know I won't like?

When you have considered your alternatives, write them down, and sort them according to priority. Now you have the beginning of a strategy that will significantly increase your chances for success.

The value of this book to you is in direct proportion to the contributions you are willing to make toward your development. Figure 1.3 on the next page will provide an opportunity to design your own personal success plan of action.

It provides a quick, simple format for you to use. Best of all, it's self-explanatory and will give you the chance to evaluate successes on a regular basis. That way changes can be made in time, so that it is possible for you to reach career objectives on schedule.

Figure 1.3
Personal Success Plan

1. Where do I stand now?
• Major Strengths • Basic Weaknesses • Important Personal Achievements to Date This Year

2. Where do I want to go?

Objectives I Can Achieve	Important to My Success Because	To Be Achieved by (date)

3. How do I get to where I want to go?

Outline of Actions to Take	Will Contribute to Success Because	Support Required	Possible Costs

4. When must I check for results?

Date Plan is to be Reviewed	Specific Results to Check	Required Revisions

Eagles Don't Flock

*A life spent digging is worth nothing if you
plant no olive trees*—SICILIAN PROVERB

The plan you complete should put this business of attaining success into a highly personal perspective. One point becomes clear immediately: maturity is the essential ingredient. Obstacles to success cannot be solved in childish ways or satisfied with adolescent experiences. Maturity involves an intelligent appraisal of failures and disappointments, as well as a balanced appreciation of the steps that lead to accomplishment.

Certainly, courage is needed in implementing any plan. In some instances, you must take a calculated risk—but there is comfort in the knowledge that relative failure in attempting great things is better than the shame of not trying.

This doesn't mean being foolish, rash, or stupid. It doesn't mean taking the one-in-a-million chance for success. It does mean balancing gain against risk and realizing that coolness under pressure is more effective than worry.

> **Schooling does not automatically deliver an education. Real learning can be tested only by adults and judged only by their performance.**

Even the most resolute among us share feelings of inadequacy before taking on a demanding task. There has never been a notable career that has not known its hour of defeat. The most astute must admit to making their quota of mistakes.

The point is that despite misgivings, despite the lump in your throat before taking on anything new for the first time, the courage to get on with it is absolutely essential for success.

You must develop an instinct for adjusting your efforts, so that the overall objective of a project or operation will be advanced. Certainly, check your plan when you can—that's always good advice; but be ready to play it by ear if that becomes necessary.

What is called for, of course, is flexibility of both mind and method. What may function smoothly today can show signs of strain tomorrow, because of some new development that could not have been foreseen.

Clarence Chamberlain, who made history by piloting the first airplane to carry a passenger across the Atlantic, found himself off course. He swooped down on a ship to see its name, looked it up in the shipping column of a newspaper he found under the seat of his plane, calculated the ship's position—and set his course for Europe.

With so much attention being paid to entrepreneurs, many of America's larger, well-established businesses have begun to recognize the potential that may exist among talented, aggressive individuals. Rather than lose such people, they have reasoned to give them more freedom and more opportunity to express their ideas in *their present positions*. Thus has been created the *intra*preneur—an individual who applies his entrepreneurial talents *within an existing organization* instead of starting a new one.

> **If you think more about yesterday than tomorrow you will have a lot of unpleasant surprises.**

Occasionally, husband and wife teams can get double benefits from working together. For example, one couple I know about built up a small electronics parts dealership, buying and selling surplus goods. As development in the electronics field increased, however, they also discovered that products became obsolete more quickly. They wrestled with the problems this situation was causing them and decided to move out in a new direction, reclaiming and recycling the precious metals used in computer and telecommunications equipment.

Instead of staying too long with a business on the way down, they took the risk and moved in a new, creative, and profitable direction.

Stick Your Neck Out

> As he was going about the time-consuming work of selecting people for his new computer company, H. Ross Perot, posted this sign in many places:
> *Eagles don't flock—you have to find them one at a time.*

Real achievers work for the satisfaction of it, because of internal goals. They don't look to committees for safe refuge. Rather, they're perfectly willing to stand out as individuals whose knowledge and opinions are to be tested. Over time, this brings a sense of inner confidence. When it is in the best interest of their organization, they will risk taking a strong position on a proposal—even when there is no chance to improve their personal standing by doing so.

Successful men and women make sure their ideas do not become inbred. That's because they spend considerable amounts of time with people who have different interests, experiences, and backgrounds. This helps them keep their own importance in perspective. It also helps them get at the real truth.

Successful people know the importance of taking a break from routine. This rotation of interest is as important to the productivity of the mind as rotation of crops is to the fertility of the soil.

Finally, successful people can laugh at themselves. In most cases, they have an infectious sense of humor, which lubricates all of their human relationships. For example, a friend of mine who has six children says this about the money he has spent on health care: "I go to what is called a family doctor. He treats mine and I support his!"

Successful People Are Used to Sacrifice

In nearly four decades as head football coach at Penn State, Joe Paterno has compiled an enviable record. Coach Paterno, who knows more about success than defeat, feels that while winning is always desirable, much can be learned from defeat. As true of football as it is of business, a major factor is the ability to look at situations realistically. Poor performance, whether from lack of motivation or training, is self-defeating because it soon affects the will to win.

Paterno is devoted to the idea that the greatest single factor involved in winning is the willingness of individuals to make personal sacrifices for the group. This includes *all* individuals—even the "stars." A competitive spirit is important, sure, but not without a deep-down sense of loyalty and responsibility. Combined they result in a commitment to an institution, a job, and those with whom one must work. The outcome?

Not just uncommon individuals but uncommon individuals *and* an unbeatable team.

> **If you expect excellence from others, you must do two things. First, know what it is. Second, show appreciation when you get it.**

Figure 1.4 shows you how to apply these principles at work, and to improve your relationship with your boss.

Figure 1.4
Surefire Ways to Please Your Boss

1. **Go above and beyond expectation.** Help your boss make it easy to decide in your favor to give you the biggest possible raise.

2. **Bring solutions, not problems.** Arguing with your associates only complicates your boss's life.

3. **Bounce back from mistakes.** Never blame someone else for your errors. When you do, things always get worse.

4. **Avoid the temptation to make excuses.** Who really cares about your problems? The only real issue is—are you accountable or aren't you?

5. **Don't depend on reminders to complete your work.** Set interim deadlines for tasks and meet them.

6. **Shoot for a good record, not perfection.** Accept the reality of some failure and learn from it.

7. **Think ahead—eliminate unpleasant surprises.** The best way to attract favorable attention to yourself and *your* boss.

8. **Don't dwell on successes.** Move quickly to new projects before compliments become shackles.

9. **Never assume your boss's goals are the same as yours without negotiating them.** Write them down—meet regularly—make each day count toward meeting them.

10. **When an agreement is reached—get going!** Those who wait to be told what to do continue to be told what to do. Their value decreases.

Before continuing, it is important that you complete your plans for success. Begin now to implement the thoughts you have had and to fulfill the commitments you've made. They provide a foundation for the ideas in the chapters that follow.

Success does not demand sensational ideas, selfish interests, monetary rewards, or grasping for power at the expense of others who may be better qualified. Instead, it requires a return to fundamental but often neglected principles.

The Unused Keys to Success summarized here, can change your life. They only require that you *put them to work*. Will you?

In Conclusion...The Unused Keys to Success

- The greatest rewards begin when we change from "What's in it for me?" to "How can I help you?"

- The best motivator of people is not money, but *genuine benefit*. If you help others, they will need you. If you help them again and again—they will need you again and again!

- To avoid failure is to limit accomplishment. Avoiding failure is not the same as success.

- Confidence grows with achievement.

- Seek responsibility. Don't hang around waiting to be told what to do.

- Be accountable. In every important assignment,

be the first to determine WHO will do WHAT by WHEN.

- Always look for *what* is wrong before *who* is wrong.
- Brainpower without willpower is no power.
- Cooperation is spelled "We!"
- Thinking is the hardest work there is. Don't avoid it.
- Competence without accomplishment is worthless. Intentions have no value without results.
- Look on the bright side. Concentrate on what *can* be done.
- As early in life as possible, learn what it is you have to give—and GIVE IT. When you do, the world will seek you out.
- Exploit yourself! Use yourself up! Wind up the day tired but not exhausted.
- SERVE!

Chapter 2

How To
Believe In Yourself

Developing Self-Confidence

The Unemployable Sales Leader

He gets up before six every morning. The pain is always there. Medicines cover his night stand. Twisted fingers make it hard to tie his shoes. He knows he's different. His mother had long ago explained how an instrument used when he was born had caused brain damage, leading to cerebral palsy, that affected his walking, talking and hand movements.

Every day is the same. It takes a lot of time, but the sixty-four-year-old is finally ready to leave for work. He wants to look good, because he knows his customers expect it. He can't drive, so heads to the nearest bus stop.

He knows most people think he's mentally impaired, so every day he must prove they are wrong.

Several government agencies have told him he was "unemployable" and offered permanent disability checks.

But Bill Porter doesn't see it that way. He's always wanted to be a salesman and that's what he does for Watkins, a home products company. As a matter-of-fact, for several years he was that company's top salesman in a four-state territory. Now he is the only one selling door-to-door in the company's 75,000 sales force. He walks over eight miles every working day.

Because he works on straight commission, there is no salary, no paid vacations, holidays, raises or health insurance. Not long ago, he had back surgery, couldn't work for five months and had to sell the house he inherited from his mother to pay debts. Undaunted, he now rents from the people who bought his house and is back on his sales route.

Bill Porter goes for it everyday. His body aches from head to toe. He stumbles, his body tilts forward so he's continually off balance. Every step is unsteady, staggering. But he believes he's proving something. He's proving that he's in charge—of his schedule, of his work, of his livelihood, of his life. And he is!

CONFIDENCE IS ONE OF THE KEYSTONES OF SUCCESS. Those who are less than optimistic about the present and future view a crisis as an unsolvable problem, an immovable obstacle, a persistent dilemma.

The Chinese, a people who have endured centuries of crisis, take the more enlightened view. In their lexigraphy the word crisis has a double meaning. It stands for danger, but it also means opportunity.

What is Confidence?

> "Great minds have purpose. Others have wishes." —WASHINGTON IRVING

The dictionary lists at least eight definitions for the word *confidence*. Perhaps the most straightforward defines this noun as "the mental attitude of trusting a person or thing."

People who display confidence in themselves, in others, and in public or private matters have certain characteristics worth examining. They are, for example, tough-minded.

They recognize, perhaps instinctively, that the affairs of men and women—whether they are in business, the arts, society, sports, or academe—are seldom forums for aimless discussion or debate. They are, rather, fields of action.

Those who don't know what they are trying to accomplish will fail. Worse yet, they frequently communicate their uncertainty to others. The result is group ineffectiveness.

There remains great truth in the anonymous adage:

"There are many paths to success, but the route to failure is clear—try to please everyone!"

Why do people vacillate? For two reasons. Tough-mindedness isn't possible when the intellectual acumen necessary for clearly analyzing a situation is lacking and the ability to formulate a plan for action is missing. There's also another possibility. Those lacking tough-mindedness don't have the persistence to see a situation through to a successful conclusion. Obviously, it's vital to believe in oneself—and to dare!

But tough-mindedness alone isn't always sufficient. Unless it is combined with flexibility, the problem of stubbornness emerges. Many men and women have innovative, workable, sometimes brilliant ideas. But they find themselves frustrated at every turn, because any change of pace or altering of plans sends them into a tailspin. Unless it's done their way, it's no way.

Chances are that deep down these people are frightfully insecure. Truly confident people see nothing wrong in a change of plans or direction, provided it continues to advance them toward goals they're convinced are worthwhile.

Confidence is also reflected in one's ability to communicate. The individual who communicates with skill often possesses the knack for saying things in a way others will remember. Equally important, this individual can say no in a way that will not cause distress or hard feelings.

Closely allied with communication is a strong memory—not for trivia, loose facts, or statistics anyone can find in a file drawer or library—but one sharpened by acute powers of observation.

Thinking—The Unused Gift

While uncertainty is associated with a lack of confidence, the two are not necessarily synonymous. Some people, when faced with an iffy situation, are stopped dead in their tracks. If a way out is not immediately available, they simply fold up and quit.

Other people shrug off uncertainty. As far as they are concerned, it is a fact of everyday life. They know it is possible to be confident and uncertain simultaneously. At one time or another everyone is likely to have genuine doubts about achieving success in an immediate situation. But as far as long range goals are concerned, they have every confidence each will be reached on schedule.

> **"All things come to those who wait—but only what's left over by those who hustle!"** Anonymous

Most people don't ask for guarantees, because they've learned there's no such thing as a sure bet—either in life or at the racetrack. There are no certainties, only possibilities. Over a period of time, odds are that probabilities will work in one's favor. Such people depend on themselves, on their surroundings, and on things they believe in. They make their own way.

Whenever they arrive at the crossroads of danger and opportunity, they quickly recognize danger, because that is the prudent thing to do. They also recognize there is a fighting chance that danger can be overcome and opportunity seized. Others who are less confident want reassurances they won't stumble—that someone will catch them should they fall—before committing themselves. Where you find weakness you will invariably find low self-confidence.

No doubt about it, the greatest gift of all is good health. Without it, life is at best misery and at worst painful death. If we are healthy, our next greatest asset is the capability to think.

Unfortunately, God gives us the *ability* to think, but does not guarantee it. Too many Americans are forgetting that basic truth. Here is a good example from today's sports page.

> A rookie football player is competing to be kept on the roster of an NFL team. The final cut is tomorrow. "It's hard," he says, "because you want to just go out and react and play your game without necessarily

having to think 'What do I have to do on this play and that play?' You just want to be able to do what comes naturally and show the coaches what kind of talent you have."

News flash: Your talent is useless, young man, if you refuse to think about how to use it!

God enabled us to think so we can reason, judge, discern, analyze, discriminate, evaluate, sift, sort, articulate, decide, reconsider and then act.

But when did you last show your gratitude for this wondrous gift? In what way? A thankful prayer perhaps? An anonymous gift? A sudden act of kindness?

How about showing your appreciation by becoming a better thinker? What better way to improve yourself and everyone around you? Why? Here are some very practical reasons. Thinking is:

- Your best protection against quacks, liars, and cheaters.

- Your best route to advancement.

- Your resistance to bad emotional decisions.

- Your removal of the blinders of prejudice.

- Your means to overcome inertia.

- Your most reliable protection from manipulators.

- Your insurance against unexpected loss.

- Your antidote for those whose charm is really venom.

- Your best bet to avoid fraud and deception.

- Your restorative power to cope with tragedy.

- Your release from the shackles of learned hate.

- Your shield against charismatic, but selfish, leaders who only want your vote.

- Your nourishment for recovery.

- Your restraint from repeating mistakes.

- Your defense against deceptive advertising.

- Your strategy to disarm those who would delude you.

- Your armor to break the arrows of those committed to cause you to fail.

- Your resistance to those who would entice you with flattery.

- Your screen for suspicious influences.

- Your tools to unlock unrealized potential.

- Your storehouse providing sustenance for hard times.

- Your stimulant to stop bad habits.

- Your discipline to build on successes.

- Your fortress of defense from unexpected attack.

- Your source for renewal.

Unused, it is the quickest route to failure. Used fully, thinking offers the most reliable pathway to success.

But, beware. Thinking is the hardest work there is. It comes easy for no one. Surely, that's why we all avoid it.

Developing an Aura of Confidence

It's all very well to emphasize the benefits and values of self-confidence. But what do confident persons do that distinguishes them? What do they look like? How do they act, and react, to the day-to-day pressures everyone faces? What kind of people are they and, just as important, how is a confident image projected? Let's look at confidence in terms of appearance, attitude, and actions.

Consider *appearance* for the moment. Persons who display an aura of confidence look the part. They're decisive. Energetic. They play the role to the hilt. Even the way they walk: rapidly, as though on a mission of importance. Their posture is arrow-straight. If they slouch, it's never where others can see them.

When seated, confident people look alert. If they ever slump, it's probably behind a closed door. The chair they choose behind their desk is modest in size, so they never appear small or trapped. Its color is neutral and is made of material that won't squeak or cling to the body.

They've learned how to detect and adapt to the style of the organization for whom they work—or with whom they are associated. If the style is relaxed and congenial, then they have no problem conforming. If it's tough and cool, then they have little difficulty playing the role. Even the way they dress suggests they're in step with the leaders of the organization.

Those who display confidence reveal it in their search for success.

They notice people, places, and things others are likely to overlook. They've attuned their senses to what others are doing, saying, and thinking. They observe, assess, study, and interpret situations to which others give scarcely a glance. That is why their timing is precise, why they are well prepared to seize the moment and its opportunities.

Confident people understand clearly how to keep a confidence. Once trust has been extended they do not violate it and risk losing loyalty. That's the reason confident people give information before it is needed, so others can make use of it in their work. To keep abreast of what's going on, they read the same publications as upper managers and pass pertinent facts along to others.

The only time the confident maintain a high degree of security and silence is when changes are occurring swiftly. Not only do they keep their cool, they also have the patience to watch and wait. They know from experience how quickly situations can change; what looked desperate yesterday may blow over tomorrow.

Another vital element of confidence is the ability to

share information; much depends on keeping every-one informed. An unusual but very effective communi-cation technique has been created at a company in Texas. The president has put the janitor's office in the executive office building. It isn't to prove how democ-ratic he is—or because the janitor is an old fishing buddy. He has a real business purpose.Whenever he wants important information to reach everyone in the company, the president walks down the hall and tells the janitor. In less than a day, everyone knows exactly what's on the boss's mind.

He used the same kind of logic when the headquar-ters building was under construction. Halls were made double their width. Not for crowd control purposes, or for hasty exits. The purpose was to allow for informal gatherings of employees. The president reasoned that was where the really important meetings take place, and that's where important decisions are finally imple-mented—not at formal meetings or in board rooms.

Most important, the confident have a knack for ask-ing the right questions. Whenever a *discrepancy* occurs, they'll ask questions such as:

- What's the difference between what's being done and what's supposed to be done?

- What is the event that causes me to say that things aren't right?

- Why am I dissatisfied?

- Is this really important? What would happen if nothing is done?

If it's a question of *performance*, the confident individual is prone to ask:

- How often is this particular skill used?
- Is regular feedback offered, so this person knows how they're doing?
- Is enough training provided?
- What would happen if we did it this person's way instead of my way?

What about *actions*? How do the confident handle them to their advantage?

First, they've learned how to concentrate their energy. They recognize that constantly working overtime is no answer.; and neither are weekends spent away from family and recreational activities. What is required is the desire to get the job done. One suggestion is to split the day into manageable segments. As chores are completed, a feeling of accomplishment grows which helps to fire-up energy, so that additional tasks can be taken on.

Confident people take responsibility. They look for problems to solve. When *obstacles* prevent desired performance, they ask:

- Does this person know what's expected?
- Are there conflicting demands on his or her time?

- Do policies or other restrictions interfere?
- What other obstacles may be blocking acceptable performance?

Even in a highly charged situation, confident people are low key. They neither speak nor act hastily. Personal emotions are held in check, so that decisions are not colored by anger, gloom, or despair.

When really upset about an event or conflict, the confident person will talk it out or act it out—alone. In this way anxiety is brought under control. What's more, time is available in which to think and act rationally. Above all, they never forget that there is no lasting relationship without mutual benefit.

Here's a verbatim example of how this suggestion might work in a real life situation:

"Jim...why did you by-pass me on that Lamont deal? You know how I feel about that company and the money problems we've had with them in the past. Your decision to go ahead without consulting me— or the other people in the department for that matter—smacks just a bit of poor policy and bad timing."

Jim pauses before answering.

"I'm really sorry you're upset Bill. Let me begin by covering the background behind the decision, as well as the timing involved. As you'll recall, we decided as a group at our last meeting to..."

In any face-to-face confrontation, make certain you're the one who picks the time and place. Never sit across from an opponent. Sit next to them or with their chair parallel to your desk—if in an office. Facing an opponent from behind a desk creates a gap that is harder to bridge.

In any disagreement, stress the positive aspects of the situation. This means being constructive. If it isn't possible to agree on several points, then suggest deferring them until later. Get points of agreement out of the way first. Then go back to the sticky ones.

In one-on-one situations, sit close to the other person. Speak lower than in normal conversation. That way the listener will have to strain slightly to hear—and as a result, is more likely to listen with greater attention.

Remember, most people want to avoid a fight. The confident individual understands this clearly and uses it to express a position right from the start. This doesn't mean being rude or overaggressive. It means starting with facts and proof that are undeniable. Should a confrontation grow heated, have a fall-back position ready. This will give you time to continue pursuing your objectives from a different tack—without making any unnecessary concessions.

Sometimes it's tough getting your point across, because the person with whom you're talking monopolizes the conversation. When that happens, you must deliver a signal that now it's your turn to talk. Here are several workable tips for doing just that.

- Put your hand gently on the other person's shoulder.

- Turn away from the other person and say something that is hardly audible. When asked to repeat your comment—jump in!

- Take advantage of any pauses in the conversation to start delivering the points you wish to express.

- Hold up your hand, then break boldly into the other person's conversation.

Experts (lawyers, accountants, consultants, bankers) will sometimes try to overwhelm you with their rhetoric. Challenge them by asking them to repeat—in lay terms—exactly what they are talking about. Not only is this a great way to pinprick a few super egos, the "experts" will be more likely to hop down from their lofty perches and talk in terms that can be understood.

Any time you trade ideas with another person, with the intention of changing relationships, or whenever you talk to reach an agreement—you're negotiating.

Because negotiating frequently demands tough bargaining before a deal can be sealed, it's important to follow some principles. One of the most vital is making sure all parties walk away from the discussion satisfied; feeling that they have gained something valuable.

Even before negotiation begins, these steps should be taken:

- **Study the matter to be negotiated**, as well as the strengths and weaknesses of your adversary.

- **Examine the setting** within which the negotiation will take place.

- **Develop a checklist** to avoid omission of any important items to cover.

- **Consider possible hidden surprises**, agendas, or new items the other side may raise.

- **Select a strategy** or game plan you will follow.

During the negotiation, keep these points in mind:

- Prepare and introduce supporting material according to the strategy you've selected.

- Make concessions only when they will count the most.

- LOOK and LISTEN to the other person's reactions to your proposals.

- Have a ready excuse for breaking off the discussion, if necessary.

- Present a win-win solution.

- Be prepared to settle when it appears certain a reasonable compromise will be accepted.

After the negotiation, there is one thing to remember:

- Don't hesitate to reopen an important issue or discuss an error in computation or fact.

Finally, a hallmark of confident people is their persistence. Setbacks, pressures, and disappointments are taken in stride so long as a single objective remains to be achieved. The story of Charles Goodyear is a great example. He was obsessed with the idea of making rubber impervious to extremes of temperature. Prior to vulcanization, rubber products became soft and sticky in summer; hard and brittle in winter.

Although he had no scientific training, and knew practically nothing about the properties of the various chemicals he mixed with rubber, Goodyear experimented endlessly. He met not only with the setbacks, which are a normal part of all experimentation, but bitter disappointment when success seemed almost within his grasp.

Imprisoned more than once for debt; his family poor and ill-nourished; faced with ridicule from friends, Goodyear persisted, even though his wife had threatened to leave if he continued.

In February 1839 Goodyear was kneading a batch of rubber into which he had mixed some sulphur, when he heard his wife approaching. Fearful of a confrontation, he tossed the batch hastily into the stove. Retrieving it later, he noticed a dramatic change. The rubber was charred like leather, but the heat and sulphur had vulcanized it. The rubber could now withstand heat and cold and still remain flexible. Goodyear's confidence in his ultimate success had paid off.

Building Self-Confidence

Everyone has reserves of strength they can tap into in times of stress or crisis. In the exercise that follows, you have an opportunity to draw up a personal balance sheet of assets and liabilities. It will then be possible to lay plans for overcoming weakness and, at the same time, build upon a foundation of strength.

Before you begin working, be sure to:

- Review carefully each of the worksheets included in the Confidence Evaluation, Figure 2.1.

- Decide what information or resources you will need to check concerning instances in which confidence (or a lack of it) played a key role.

- Obtain an objective picture of yourself by accurately answering all the questions.

- Recall specific instances when your confidence made possible opportunities that might otherwise have remained hidden—and when a faltering confidence not only compounded a problem, but lost the main chance as well.

Then proceed as follows:

- Note your observations and comments in the appropriate spaces of the Personal Fact Base.

- Analyze strengths on which to capitalize and weaknesses to overcome as you review Personal Assets/Liabilities. What do these revelations say about you as a person? A leader? A team member? What actions do these revelations suggest?

- Indicate the goals, both immediate and long-range, you feel are necessary to achieve in order to stimulate the growth of personal confidence.

- Check the completed worksheet on a regular basis to determine the progress being made in the development of your confidence.

Remember—there is no time limit. This exercise will benefit you most if you proceed slowly, deliberately, and thoughtfully.

FIGURE 2.1
CONFIDENCE EVALUATION WORKSHEET

PERSONAL FACT BASE			
Step 1: Answer each of the questions below as accurately and objectively as possible.			
Checkpoint	**Comment/ Strength or Weakness**	**Checkpoint**	**Comment/ Strength or Weakness**
What concept do I have of myself? (Aggressive, shy, etc.)		What kinds of problems, people, or situations scare me most? Why?	
Where do I excel?		In what situations do I display the greatest confidence?	
Where do I feel inadequate?		Do I look for what's wrong with me, before what's wrong with others?	
In what areas am I weak or ignorant?		Am I too security-conscious? Do I know why?	
What do I need to to know or do in order to grow?		Did I start achieving early in life? Explain.	
What constraints are there on my time?		What is there about failure I fear the most?	
What are my immediate objectives?		Are there any responsibilities I consciously try to avoid? Why do I?	
What are my long-range objectives?		Do I consider myself mature? Immature? Often irresponsible?	
Which of the above objectives should I undertake first? Why?		Why do I feel this way about myself?	

Figure 2.1 (continued)

Review Personal Assets/Liabilities

Step 2: In the spaces below note major strengths upon which you can capitalize, as well as weaknesses you must overcome, if your CONFIDENCE is to grow.

Areas of expertise and strengths I can use to increase my confidence. (Examples: good at making decisions, knowledge of basic job skills, etc.)	Areas in which improvement is necessary if my confidence is to improve. (Examples: inability to manage myself, find it difficult to cooperate with others, etc.)

Goals and Timetable for Achievement

Step 3: Based on a review of your personal assets and liabilities, develop a list of *specific* IMMEDIATE and LONG-RANGE OBJECTIVES you believe are essential for improving your confidence posture.

Immediate Objectives (Within the next three months)	How will you achieve them? (School, training, assuming more responsibilities, etc.)	When will you achieve them? (Specific date)
Long-Range Objectives (Between now and the end of the year)	**How will you achieve them?**	**When will you achieve them?** (Specific date)

Follow-Up Is the Key

Those who are easily defeated have hundreds of reasons why things won't work when all they need is one reason why it *will!*

Unless you follow up on a consistent basis, a program aimed at improving self-confidence can quickly become stymied.

It is one thing to carefully note areas where new growth is indicated, and quite another to get underway so that improvements can be realized. The longer any self-improvement program is delayed, the greater the chances it will never start.

There is another temptation: to spend time on the things you already do well and neglect the things you don't like or handle poorly. The Confidence Evaluation Worksheets you've just completed touch on the qualities and skills your experiences suggest are of prime importance. **By constantly checking personal performance, it is possible to remedy most shortcomings.** The following suggestions will help you to follow up:

- Make a *non-negotiable* commitment to yourself that you will improve your self-confidence.

- Get the help you need by joining a club, enrolling in school, volunteering your services to an organization, assisting on a committee, or taking on a new job assignment.

- Concentrate on those areas where you know your

self-confidence is weak. If, for example, you fear speaking before others, then get the training necessary. Join a club or other organization where you will be called on frequently to address the group.

- Review and evaluate progress toward goals. Check your schedule. Are you on target? If not, do you know why, or what is holding you up?

- Maintain a positive attitude about yourself so you'll be encouraged to grow and develop greater convictions and beliefs that will strengthen your self-confidence.

Lending a Hand to Others

> The worst form of employee dishonesty is not pilfering money or goods, absenteeism, or sloppy workmanship. The worst offense is to allow the boss to make a mistake that you could have prevented.

A definite self-improvement program builds confidence, no question about that. And it overcomes discouragement as well. But when you help others develop and maintain self-confidence, you become even more capable and adequate. Not only is there satisfaction in knowing that you have lent a helping hand to others, but you also reinforce the know-how and skills you've developed in a highly practical way.

When you observe friends, family, or acquaintances whose potential is being diminished because of wavering confidence or who are frequently overwhelmed with self-doubts, you have an opportunity to set them straight. True, you can't impose a program of self-improvement on anyone, but you can make yourself available.

- You can help them clarify a situation by discussing it openly.

- You can point out possible avenues to a solution, or pinpoint a problem that may be inhibiting progress.

- You can offer counsel on the best approaches to take.

- You can suggest immediate action that can help bring a problem or a situation under control.

Achievement breeds more confidence: confidence breeds more achievement. Figure 2.2 demonstrates this cycle.

The single most important ability is accountability.

Figure 2.2
The Confidence Circle

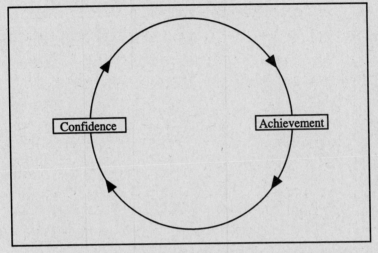

Too many people limit themselves with self-doubt and allow negative feelings to overcome them. It is possible for you to help them correct these oversights. Here are some confidence-building tips:

1. Underscore your attributes, because they form the foundation upon which a strong sense of confidence is built.

2. Learn to analyze situations, so that an intelligent plan can be conceived to capitalize on your pluses and minimize your minuses.

3. Learn to be your own best critic by clarifying your motives with the person who knows you best; stating your position in writing; and answering ques-

tions such as, "If I'm right, what do I really gain?" "Does anyone else win?" "If so, are they aware of it, and is it important to them?"

4. Anticipate resistance likely to be encountered in a situation. You will be better able to work confidently toward an accommodation acceptable to all.

5. Combine tough mindedness with flexibility.

6. Face situations and personalities squarely, particularly those that frighten you off. Take them on by confronting them with cold facts and logic.

7. Refuse to be defeated by momentary setbacks. Take the long-range view. It's what is finally achieved that counts.

8. Maintain an optimistic attitude. Not only will it buoy your spirits, but it has a confidence-inspiring effect on others.

9. Sharpen your ability to observe accurately and to communicate what you've seen and learned **objectively**.

10. Make full use of the ideas you uncovered in your Confidence Evaluation Worksheets.

11. Review your progress constantly, so that personal liabilities can be converted into positive assets.

One final thought: self-confidence must show a sensitivity toward human values, not only for the good of others but for our own peace of mind. We do this best by building our relationships on each person's strong points, so that we are not blinded by their limitations.

Before proceeding, make certain the worksheets in this chapter have been completed, tested, and tried in your own situation.

In Conclusion...Make Yourself Needed

- Learn to be flexible in areas where moral values are not at stake. Very few things in life can be done only one way.

- Remember, to avoid failure is to limit accomplishment. Avoiding failure is not the same as success.

- Teach yourself to be persistent. Stay with important assignments. Outlast your competition. Back away only when you can be convinced that other important opportunities are being lost or you are risking your health.

- Don't waste time on things that won't matter anyway.

- Experiment in low-risk areas. Don't worry about embarrassment. Don't be ashamed to be different. Criticism of those who try new ways is mostly envy.

- Learn to be your own best critic by clarifying your motives with the person who knows you best; stating your position in writing; and answering these questions: "If I'm right, what do I really gain?" "Does anyone else win?" "If so, are they aware of it, and is it important to them?"

- Keep in mind that confidence grows with achievement. Plan carefully and each step will seem easier.

- Match yourself with opportunities that are appropriate for you. Bluffing is advisable only in poker, and then only if you can afford it!

Chapter 3

YOUR VALUES ARE SHOWING

Cafeteria Now Open for Values, Virtues, and Integrity

THE WORDS VALUES, VIRTUES, AND INTEGRITY HAVE entered the political arena...big time. Unfortunately, the accusations and arguments have served only to cloud their original meanings and make most Americans more confused than ever about their personal interpretations.

The most fascinating aspect of this confusion for me is that too many of us seem to have made all values relative, all virtues temporary, and integrity irrelevant.

If **values** refer to our personal scale of worth, if **virtues** are related to our sense of moral excellence, and if **integrity** reflects our moral honesty—we are facing some very powerful questions. Our individual and collective answers will have a more powerful impact on the future of our country than any specific social or political issue. Woven into the answers are the fibers that bind us together as a nation. What is your view?

- Should values be selected from a menu posted for today? Or should certain standards prevail continuously?

- What makes virtues meaningful in everyday living?

- Does integrity really matter?

- How effective are the teachings of our historic Judeo-Christian morality?

- How are values, virtues, and integrity taught and learned? If mostly in childhood from exemplary parents, we have cut our potential number of role models in half with a fifty-percent divorce rate!

William Bennet, in his *Book of Virtues*, identifies ten categories for virtuous behavior: self-discipline, compassion, responsibility, friendship, work, courage, perseverance, honesty, loyalty, and faith. In it, he speaks of "moral literacy" and the importance of transmitting it to the young.

The importance of this challenge to each generation was underscored long ago by Plato in his *Republic*: "Anything received into the mind of a child," he said, "is likely to become indelible and unalterable and, therefore, it is most important that the tales which the young first hear should be models of virtuous thoughts."

There is far too much evidence that the currently living heirs to this challenge are shamefully ignoring it.

- We are too preoccupied satisfying our *current* desires.

- We are ignoring the consequences of immoral behavior on future generations.

- We are seeking more and more entitlements from government and are less and less willing to share. For example:

> As government welfare programs spread, they tend to lessen the individual taxpayer's sense of guilt for not helping the needy person-to-person. Fact: A recent study revealed that the tiny nation of Sri Lanka has the highest "comfort index" among Third World countries. Its citizens average only 2,000 calories a day, but ninety percent of them are literate.

> The former head of the National Conference of Catholic Charities has said, "When the proponents of the new public welfare reach their utopia, there will no longer be a place for religion in the American community."

Kenneth Starr, whose panel is investigating suspicious events at the highest level of the federal government cites President James Madison's views on what civic virtue meant to our founding fathers. They hoped, he says, "that individuals, as they pursued their self-interested goals would feel a commitment to justice, to civility, and above all, to truthfulness. Without these traits, the individual cannot be a true citizen. And without virtuous citizens," the founders believed, "self-government will ultimately self-destruct."

Conclusion: The stakes are very, very high if virtuous behavior is not taught and values are ignored.

In their new book *The Fourth Turning*, historians William Strauss and Neil Howe summarize what we must do as a nation to become a society of shared values that work in the twenty-first century. They believe that as a society, we should begin now to:

	Action Needed
• **Clean up the culture.**	When events force a decadent society to mobilize, the result can be facism.
• **Simplify.**	Shrink government now to make room for growth during a crisis, when America will need public authority again.
• **Team up.**	Stress duties over rights. Use technology to bring people together.
• **Prepare youth.**	Teach civic habits and group skills, shift government benefits away from the non-needy old and toward the needy young.

Individuals, they believe, should:

	Action Needed
• **Strengthen family ties.**	Kinship will be the ultimate safety net for health and old age; government will have other priorities.
• **Safeguard reputation.**	Classic virtues like loyalty and civic honor will be newly-prized by neighbors and public officials.

We must realize that integrity does not break suddenly. It crumbles gradually and disappears.

Without prevailing moral standards we have no civility, just boorishness and meaningless entitlements.

You hear it everywhere: "Don't mess with me." "None of your business." "Get out of my way." "I don't see a waiting line." "I was here first." "No one was around, so I took it." "Back off!"

- Drivers deliberately run over people.

- Kids shoot other kids for their sneakers.

- Live-in males abuse and murder their "woman's" infant because it cries.

- A mother seeks revenge on the girl who made the cheerleading squad instead of her daughter.

- Date rape is so rampant, a special drug is advertised to control it.

- Entrance to inner-city colleges is guaranteed... even if you are functionally illiterate.

- Cheating on exams is considered okay, since so many do it.

- A high school teacher gives his students competing in a contest answers, so they won't feel inferior and can win a prize.

Our tolerance has gone too far. We're beyond rudeness and crudeness, and into foulness and shame. We've lost our sense of consistency. We can't laugh at Dennis Rodman's perforated body, multi-colored hair, and outlandish dress one minute—and then act as if his uncontrolled mouth and temper are insignificant when he kicks a bystander and is expelled from a game for which he is paid millions.

- Behavior matters.

- Rules matter.

- Self-control matters.

- Other people's rights matter.

If life is intended to be either a continuous masquerade or a license to please only ourselves, where are the benefits of freedom? Some freedom is then lost in a maze of confusion and chaos. At worst, it is continuous conflict. At best, it is limbo. We can't continue on a course where new prisons are the fastest growing industry in twenty-five percent of the states.

The basketball club that employs a Dennis Rodman should not call itself a team. No real team allows one player license to follow his personal preferences. No coach or team member can ever be comfortable wondering if the volatile, untrustworthy, loose cannon mate will be there when they need him most.

General Colin Powell believes he is a living example of how durable values begin at home. His began "with understanding the difference between right and wrong" taught by his parents and extended via "faith in God and a belief in the rewards of hard work, education and self-respect."

Integrity blends our virtuous beliefs with the values expressed by our daily actions. It is evaluated constantly by every one we meet. But only we can alter it. The first step is to ask yourself:

- What do I want said about me when I'm gone? What do I want people to remember and talk about? How I looked? What I wore? Whom did I influence? Was it good? Was it bad? Was it neutral?

- Was I honest? Deceitful? Generous? Stingy?

- What instances or examples of my character do they recall?

- Was I a thankful person? How did I show it?

- Was I arrogant or humble?

- Was I trusting or suspicious?

- Was I friendly or aloof?

- Was I an accumulator or a giver?

- Was I more concerned about people or things?

Are you curious how people who know you would describe you? How would it compare to what you want them to see and believe?

How about those you met recently? What do they see? What impresses them? What turns them off?

If you suspect that what you want is not what people see—what will you do?

Who is Worthy of Loyalty?

There is no doubt that loyalty is never automatic. It must be earned. But how do we decide who deserves our loyalty?

Effectiveness at work requires both leaders and followers. Teams can't decide *everything*. Often they are not prepared, or simply don't have the time. But what boss is worthy of loyalty? Experience has taught me these requirements:

1. **Worthy leaders prepare well for their position.** Managing is a separate profession or career. People who want to take on a leadership position need to prepare well and continue to grow in office. Good managers are not born, they are made.

2. **Worthy leaders rate themselves and others** *objectively.* Managers who are subjective about themselves will be subjective in their evaluations of other people. Managers must be objective in their evaluations and decisions. They must know themselves well.

3. **Worthy leaders initiate change.** Organizations can get hardening of the arteries. Wise leaders know the importance of changing before you have to. They also pay close attention to hiring people who do not resist change.

4. **Worthy leaders work from the inside out.** The most meaningful change begins inside yourself. If you say you believe in promotion from within, you have to devote time and money to helping people develop. You have to plan ahead for who you are going to have in your key leadership positions and why.

5. **Worthy leaders manage expectations.** Effective managers clarify expectations regularly. You can't just have a plan, put it in a drawer, and hope it works. You must have a way of linking expectation with delivery. I call it **Performance Based Management** (PBM).

6. **Worthy leaders are good teachers.** Good teachers are good role models—they practice what they teach. Inconsistency kills initiative. Managers who are good teachers are accessible. They do not depend upon edicts, memos, or even voice mail. They're constantly engaged in a process of cutting, fitting, sifting, and sorting to arrive at the best solutions. They create well-informed teams at all levels. They concentrate on preventing problems. They

praise and acknowledge the behind-the-scenes people who are usually taken for granted. They weed out those who aren't carrying their load.

7. **Worthy leaders recognize real value.** They quickly discover who gets the best results. They determine who can accept constructive criticism. They realize if you bring people along too fast, they never learn to handle opposition and criticism.

8. **Worthy leaders are management incubators.** Where do you incubate managers? Who are the people responsible for incubating future leaders? Identify these places, nurture them, and reward those responsible for them.

9. **Worthy leaders provide opportunity for personal growth.** They are not afraid of having strong, even aggressive people reporting to them. They realize that every important project or goal needs a champion—not a committee, but an individual. Leaders must think carefully about what they champion and how critical that project is.

10. **Worthy leaders reward accomplishment—not mediocrity.** People should be able to feel that their success is directly related to the success of their leaders.

> **Leaders must not only be willing to share credit—they must do it! They must show by their actions how much they want their team members to succeed.**

Reality Check: Do You Want to Be What You Are or What You Can Become?

- Your beliefs determine your convictions.
- Your convictions determine your satisfactions.
- Your thoughts determine your actions.
- Your habits make you predictable.
- Your character determines your future.
- Your work defines your legacy.

Ask yourself:

- Do I agree with these statements?
- If yes—what changes in your daily living are called for?
- If no—write your own version of the relationship between beliefs, convictions, thoughts, habits, character, and work.

Chapter 4

How To Learn From Your Mistakes

Converting Problems Into Opportunities

The young amateur had a slight lead at the seventeenth hole in a very tight golf tournament. His drive had dropped just short of the green and, if his luck held, chances were good he could "birdie" the hole.

As he walked down the fairway toward his ball, he stopped suddenly in dismay. The ball had rolled into the bottom of a paper bag someone in the gallery had carelessly discarded.

Here was a problem, which unless solved immediately, could cause him to blow his lead. What could he do?

The young man studied the situation carefully for several minutes, and then acted.

Taking a book of matches from his pocket, he set the paper bag afire. When it was reduced to ashes, he selected an appropriate iron and swung. The ball lofted, rolled to the lip of the cup and dropped in.

MOST GOLFERS—PERHAPS EVEN SOME PROS—MIGHT have shrugged, taken a penalty, and passed it off with the comment that it was "just another break of the game." Not everyone would take the time to calmly identify and define the dimensions of the problem. In their anxiety they might not always look at a problem from a number of different aspects. Few might study the situation to see what creative possibilities existed to reach the best practical solution under the circumstances.

Certainly the story of the young golfer illustrates dramatically the need to be calm under pressure, and to stick with the problem until solved. His persistence demonstrated a willingness to concentrate his energy and intensity to resolve a situation that could cost him the lead in the tournament.

The life of Abraham Lincoln offers an excellent example of persistence paying off, despite great adversity. In 1832 he lost his job and was defeated for the

Illinois legislature. He failed in business in 1833. His sweetheart died in 1835. He suffered a nervous break-down in 1836. He was defeated for Speaker of the Illinois House in 1838. He was defeated for nomination to Congress in 1843. He lost his re-nomination for Congress in 1848. He was rejected for land officer in 1849. He was defeated for the U.S. Senate in 1854. He was defeated for nomination for vice president of the United States in 1856 and was again defeated for the U.S. Senate in 1858.

In 1860 Abraham Lincoln became the sixteenth president of the United States.

> **The only people who can justify thinking more about yesterday than tomorrow are historians.**

The problem pyramid (Figure 4.1 on page 98) offers revealing percentages concerning those who seek... solve...avoid ...or who ARE the problem. Where do you fit in?

What's Your Problem?

> **Ideas, like people, are not born great. They are mixed gradually by persistence, time, and hard work. Very few can be stalked and trapped.**

FIGURE 4.1
THE PROBLEM PYRAMID

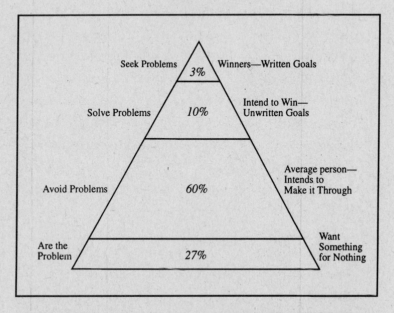

Louis Houck had a contract to build a railroad line from Cape Giradeau to Delta, Missouri. To fulfill the contract and get paid for the job, a train had to reach Delta by January 1, 1881.

Houck purchased used rails on credit from a competitor. Work progressed smoothly, until the tracks were within a mile of Delta. Then his supplier refused to sell him any more rails. With no other rails available and the deadline rapidly approaching, it looked as though Mr. Houck had an unsolvable problem on his hands.

On December 30, 1880, Houck and his crew loaded railroad ties onto the train. At the crack of dawn on

December 31 they ran the train to the end of the existing track. Working swiftly, they tore out several hundred feet of track from behind the parked train and moved those rails to the new ties laid out in front of the train. Once the rails were secured to the ties, the train was moved up to the end and the process was repeated.

Just before midnight, Houck's train pulled into the station at Delta. He had beaten the deadline and secured the railroad right-of-way. His hard work and unconventional thinking paid off in a situation in which others might have quit.

> **What I need is somebody to make me do what I can do.** —Ralph Waldo Emerson

When you sense something isn't right, you always have two choices. You can ignore the situation, in which case there's nothing to worry about because you don't plan to do anything about it anyway; or you can make the effort to do something, which is acknowledgment that a remedy must be found.

In general, there is no problem unless the solution will have importance far greater than doing nothing at all. There is no problem if it will never be important to anyone now, or in the future. (You can probably count instances such as these on the fingers of one hand.) Most often, however, when you're hit with a problem, a solution is required in a hurry.

Why, then, is it so difficult getting started? First there is the very human tendency to sidestep troublesome issues in the hope that they'll fade away. Because we are usually pressed for time, we try to ignore the situation or, better yet, wait for others to take it on. Another difficulty is that we can get confused by the problem itself and cannot apply relevant knowledge to the situation. Unless what is wrong is immediately apparent, we're a bit uncertain about how to proceed.

Another obstacle to solving a problem is the habit of looking at every situation in the same way. There's a tendency to generalize too much. We're likely to select only that evidence that fits our preconceived notions, ideas, or opinions.

Sometime ago, a young clerk in a hardware store became concerned about the thousands of dollars worth of inventory that went unsold month after month. He knew his job was at stake if something wasn't done about it and business didn't improve soon. He suggested to the owner that they have a sale and display all the oldest items at ten cents.

The sale was so successful he got permission to have another one. It too worked out well. Now the young clerk was convinced he had what was needed to manage a store of his own. He would sell only nickel and dime items and his boss would supply the financial backing. His boss rejected the proposal, but the clerk went ahead on his own. His name—F.W. Woolworth.

Years later, his old boss recalled that every word he used in turning Woolworth down cost him about a million dollars.

Failure to reason systematically—or to complete a chain of reasoning—prevents us from shifting from one formulation of a problem to another. This makes it difficult to probe for fundamental causes. We are likely to assume that one event is a result of another, even though evidence of this fact may be lacking.

Problems are often compounded because of a failure to speak up. We hesitate because of someone's position—their clout; the delicacy of the problem itself; or the fear of hurting someone's feelings. The result is an unsolved problem that feeds on itself, and in the process grows completely out of proportion.

A severe problem can generate such a sense of urgency that sound judgment suffers. If intense enough, we can act rashly rather than rationally. One reason, perhaps, is that we tend to look at a problem in a highly personal way, instead of checking its effect on family, on friends, or on an organization.

Another reason we avoid problems is the fear we won't look good, especially around a so-called expert. We'd rather bury the problem than expose our ignorance, inexperience, or uncertainty. What happens? The problem remains stalled and generates other problems. The same holds true for a distasteful situation. The longer it sits untended, the greater the fear and tension.

Identifying and overcoming problems requires talent and practice. It is a skill few people come by naturally. Despite the fact all of us have been exposed to a variety of experiences in life, it doesn't necessary follow that the ability to reach practical solutions to problems has also been acquired.

When hit by a problem, there's the temptation to do something NOW! We feel action is so urgent, we don't take the time to get the information upon which to base judgments. Instead we rely on personal beliefs or experiences as the final authority. We may even waste time trying to find the right answer, when we should be trying to determine the nature of the problem itself. Unless we can break through surface symptoms, it isn't always possible to come to grips with what's actually wrong.

Identify What's Wrong

Before headway can be made in reaching a solution, it is necessary first to *pinpoint* the real problem. This may sound naïve, but it is often the most difficult task, because the actual problem is buried beneath the surface.

Take the case of the brand manager at Procter & Gamble who was responsible for Charmin toilet paper.

Whenever a customer complains to Procter & Gamble, the problem lands in the lap of a brand manager for a solution. The manager is expected to take whatever steps are necessary to make the customer happy. Here's the situation. Toilet paper is designed for three types of dispensers: the kind found in public washrooms, the kind typically mounted on the bathroom wall at home, and the old-fashioned kind that fits into a semicylindrical wall cavity. It seems that rolls of Charmin were just a bit too thick to fit into the old-fashioned type of dispenser.

Procter & Gamble had no intention of cutting back on the number of sheets simply to reduce the size of the rolls. Instead, the brand manager got together with personnel for engineering and research and development, and together they came up with an idea for tooling a machine that would wind paper faster, thereby reducing the diameter of the roll so that it fit easily into the dispenser.

In this situation, the Procter & Gamble staff followed several steps to bring the problem into focus. These steps can be helpful to everyone:

1. **Analyze the Situation**

    -   Contact those who are involved with the problem or who have brought the matter to your attention. Remember, few problems are ever solved long-distance.

    -   Investigate every aspect of the situation as candidly as possible. You can do this best by keeping an open mind, free of any personal bias or unrealistic expectations.

- As you observe...question! Ask about the who, what, when, where, why, and how of the situation. Verify your observations by checking with reliable witnesses.

- Look for factors surrounding the problem. Find out what caused the problem in the first place, what has resulted from the problem, who or what has been affected.

- Evaluate what you hear and see by making notes of important points.

2. **Isolate Key Factors**

- Is the problem composed of several smaller problems that can be handled separately? Even when only one big problem exists, it may be worked on more efficiently if broken down into smaller parts that are taken on one at a time.

- Limit the problem by concentrating on those elements within the scope of your authority. Can you handle them alone or do you need help?

3. **Put the Problem in Writing**

- Develop a tentative statement of the problem. This will help to keep your mental processes on target and serve as a general guide as you work toward a solution. In the statement, include such facts as:

The kind of problem it is—whether it involves a personality, a mechanism, an organization, a function, an operation, etc.

The problem's critical element—what must first be changed before anything else can be done.

The reason(s) why the problem should be solved—what will be the costs in terms of time, money, personnel, and effort; and is it worth it?

The more complex a problem, the greater the need for stating it simply. It is possible, of course, that a tentative definition may have to be altered as you progress, but you will need some basic guidelines to follow.

Get the Facts

It is foolish to attempt a solution without sufficient facts. Equally foolish is yielding to the temptation to stack facts in favor of a single approach.

As facts about the problem are collected, organize them in a form that will help you make sense of them and identify possible relationships between them. It is also important to note whether the source used is:

- Reliable—evidence that can be verified, such as readings for precision instruments, controlled experiments, etc.

- Probably reliable—comments and observations from competent, on-the-scene witnesses.

- Doubtful—hearsay, assumptions, opinions based on second-hand observations.

The amount of information to gather depends on the nature of the problem and the amount of time available. However much time may be required, remember few mistakes are ever made because too much is known.

Decide What Facts You Need

Some people are problem bringers, others are problem seekers—and a few are problem causers. Here's a case in point:

A badly-battered knight returned to his castle after a terrific battle. His armor was dented, his helmet askew, his face bloody, his horse limping, and he was almost falling out of his saddle. The lord of the castle, seeing the knight coming, hastened out to meet him. "What hath befallen you, Sir Knight?"

Straightening himself in the saddle as best he could, the knight replied, "Sire, I have labored dutifully in your service, pillaging all your enemies to the west."

"But I have no enemies to the west," replied the startled nobleman.

"Oh," said the knight. Then, after an uncomfortable pause, he continued, "Well, Sire, you surely do now!"

Never settle for assumptions on any point when it is possible to obtain specific, factual, and current data. Write down the facts as they affect the problem. This will help you determine:

- Whether or not you have a sufficient body of facts with which to work.

- If the facts reinforce information already on hand.

- The need for additional facts to fill in gaps in the information base.

- What facts to discard because they are duplications, out-of-date, or do not apply.

- How best to revise your list, so that the most important facts are at the top of your list for easy identification.

The practical steps taken in everyday planning by one of the biggest sales earners in United States history holds a lesson for everyone. Perhaps the major benefit of his planning technique is its simplicity—and the fact that the steps work. Here is a summary of his approach.

First, get an early start every day—no later than 8:00 a.m. This gives you additional hours in which to get important work accomplished.

Next, list all the sales calls to be made. That way you'll have a clearer idea of the time required for each call, as well as reminding you of the objectives to be achieved with each account.

Under every call to be made, list all the questions for which an answer is sought. Relate them to the product, but make sure they also include problems to be solved and opportunities to be identified.

Then, seek out answers. Problem-solving is what selling is all about. Solutions are what customers *really* buy.

Friendships with customers should always be sought, there's no question about that. But remember, being a buddy of a decision maker is no substitute for service, reliability, or answers to problems. That's what keeps an account alive, active, and on your side.

Evaluate to Reach a Solution

It is possible, with enough facts, to exercise creative judgment in solving a problem. While it is always desirable to reach a satisfactory solution as quickly as possible, jumping to conclusions can be extremely costly. To avoid this danger, develop as many solutions as possible. List even the absurd ones, along with those that appear to be plausible. The more possibilities listed, the less risk there is in settling on a mediocre rather than a superior solution.

As you weigh your decision, many solutions will come to mind. Talk them over with others. Their ideas will provide additional clues as to possible actions to take. The more ideas under consideration, the fresher your viewpoint will be. Better than that, you increase the chance that the solution finally selected will be the best possible one under the circumstances.

During this thinking period, look for patterns and circumstances surrounding the problem, and identify the causes of the difficulty. But avoid making criticisms that might shut off the flow of ideas—especially in discussions with others. If the problem is particularly complex, take occasional breaks to rejuvenate the creative juices and to let your ideas crystallize.

Put Solutions to the Test

Up to this point, problem-solvers have suspended judgments, even though the temptation may be great to select a single solution they've secretly favored all along. The key in testing each potential solution is *objectivity*—and a precise means of measurement. Each solution should be judged separately, in terms of its suitability, feasibility, and acceptability.

It isn't unusual to use a temporary solution to provide extra time to work on one that will be permanently implanted. But, there is a double danger in doing so. If not carefully watched and timed, the temporary solution will be bronzed—permanently. The other danger is that a temporary solution can hide the real problem.

Similar to the temporary solution is the one that doesn't quite work. The trouble is, you can't really tell whether you're dealing with an "almost" solution that will never get off the ground or a sound one that needs only a bit more tinkering to be effective.

Situations such as these occur frequently when the solution looks logical and simple—perhaps too simple! The more effective solution may prove tougher to enact, demand extra time and energy, and take longer to achieve success. So, the quick fix is substituted for the more demanding, but needed, option.

Unquestionably, every solution must be tested. Skill, imagination, and foresight are important factors in testing and there is one other vital ingredient—common sense.

Take the case of the engineer who calculated that he needed a fifty-cubic-yard concrete foundation under a support. He then proceeded to blast out fifty cubic yards of solid rock into which he poured the cement.

Imagine spending thousands of dollars blasting a huge hole and then filling it with cement, when Mother Nature had already provided the most lasting foundation of all—solid bedrock!

The engineer's actions hardly put him in contention for a Nobel prize, and the boss of the project undoubtedly had a number of unkind comments when he discovered the extra expense and such a total lack of common sense.

Devise a Standard of Measurement

An excellent rule of thumb is to avoid selecting any solution until it has been tested and proved. It'll also help to talk over the list of possible solutions you've developed with others. Frequently they can bring to light factors you may never have considered, or recommend approaches you may have overlooked.

Base your solution on three factors:

1. **Practicality**—Will it achieve the desired results?

2. **Costs**—Can we afford it?

3. **Feasibility**—Is it likely to happen?

After listing all the solutions you've tested, rate each one according to its *excellence, desirability,* or *inability* to do much in the way of saving the situation. It is possible one solution will stand out clearly above all others, but that is not likely. Most times it isn't that simple. Few solutions ever come through as exactly the best possible. Typically, a solution may score well in some areas, and flunk miserably in others.

The best solution will probably turn out to be a combination of several solutions you've tested. Ideally, the solution selected will reflect the strong points of one, reinforced by values from a number of others. The aim is to come up with one that's not only workable, but the best possible under the circumstances. Indeed, after introducing the solution, it's quite likely the best solution may have to be modified in light of changing circumstances.

Get to Work—and Follow Up

In the final step of problem-solving, the solution is put to work, and follow-up procedures are introduced. This latter step is essential, for without it you may be unable to tell whether the solution is working as anticipated.

If the problem vanishes when you put the solution into effect, you know you were right on target. But if the problem persists, then what? Don't panic. There is still time to change, revise, modify, or strengthen the solution as necessary. After reading the case of Ted Smith below, write down every solution that occurs to you, even those you feel certain have little chance for success. You're seeking as many possibilities as you can.

Solving the Seemingly Unsolvable Situation

Ted Smith is an excellent salesman with an outstanding sales record. Bob Shaw, his sales manager, called him in one day for a discussion concerning the need for realignment of Ted's territory. The conversation finally wound up as follows.

"You cut one inch from my territory and it's all yours! I mean it, Bob. I'll quit. I didn't bust my buns building this territory from scratch only to have the company rip me off just when it's getting profitable for me."

The real trouble is economics and demography. They have moved in on Ted's territory. As a result, there are now more people, industries, and opportunities than a single salesman can handle effectively. Shaw is also well aware that if Ted does decide to call it quits, major customers are likely to follow him. Equally important, competition is certain to bring in not one, but several, pros to sell and service accounts—regardless of what decision is finally reached.

The sales manager would seem to be backed into one of those classic no-win situations. Before giving up and going along with Ted, what options might you, as sales manager, want to consider? How might you bring the problem under control? Here's how Bob Shaw went about seeking a solution. He asked himself these questions:

1. Have I faced facts? This is a tough situation requiring a practical, yet unique, approach.

2. Have I checked for the new and different? What elements in this situation can be changed? Revised? Exaggerated? Turned around?

   - Can Ted be adequately compensated for any loss in income? An override arrangement perhaps? Or a percentage of sales a new salesperson might write?

   - What about a promotion? If Ted's so great, he might be good manager material. Does he possess the necessary qualities? Can he be trained?

Does the idea have any special appeal for him?
How might the company react to this idea?

- Should Ted be dumped? What will it cost to
  replace him in lost sales? Good will? Customers?
  Lowered morale among members of the sales
  staff? Competitive advantages that will disap-
  pear once a winner has left the scene?

- How about timing? Is it possible for competition
  to move in quickly and begin snapping up both
  new and old customers? How long could this
  territory remain vacant before competition fills
  the vacuum?

At this point, think about possible alternatives—the
more difficult the problem, the more you'll need. Alternatives may also be necessary to implement the final
solution successfully, because of personalities involved, time requirements, changing circumstances, and
so forth.

Most people attempt to solve problems from only
one direction or point of view. Frequently, unorthodox
thinking will lead to better solutions. At the very least,
the process itself can be enlightening.

The best way to solve a problem is simply to back-
track, asking—are the criteria used in testing solutions
appropriate?

Re-evaluate. It is possible a critical piece of information was inadvertently discarded or overlooked. To gain
a different slant, scan all the data with greater care.

Has the problem been correctly identified in the first place? Few activities are as worthless as attempting to solve the wrong problem.

What about *timing*? Was the solution introduced too soon? Too late? Should it be postponed? Have unforeseen events adversely affected the outcome of the solution?

Try to pinpoint precisely what seems to be wrong. A good way is to *interview* those involved with the problem for their reactions, ideas, and opinions. Looking for yourself remains, of course, the most effective way to determine the problem's persistence.

If no light dawns after this much checking, chances are the problem was incorrectly defined. The solution is wrong, because the problem itself was not properly stated.

The temptation to try untested shortcuts can sometimes prove overwhelming. The solution offered seems too simple. The results promised are too spectacular. The effort required, practically sweatless.

That's the situation Harold S. Geneen faced several years ago at ITT, when he found himself being urged to adopt some of the theories being advocated by the most prominent business schools in the country. His response was to challenge his managers by asking them: (1) whether the theory would motivate them personally to grow their part of the business, (2) how it would affect the people who reported to them and at bedrock, and (3) how it would meet the test of performance as related to goals.

Geneen did not believe in rigidly applying theories and formulas to management. Rather, he counseled his managers not to look for easy routes, but to be thorough in gathering facts and pay constant attention to what is happening.

All too often, so-called scientific management depends on the use of sophisticated computers and other hi-tech tools. In reality, because we never know for certain that we are right, our decisions ultimately must be based on our individual and collective reservoir of experience, exposure, and *lifelong learning*.

Solve Only the Profitable Problems

"I laid down the law," a business executive said recently. "I told my people there is a difference between solving problems because they're problems and solving problems because it's profitable for us to do so. The difference is survival. I legislated that from now on, we are going to accept only profitable problems. We'll be happy to let our competition handle the rest."

"When we did that (solve only profitable problems)," another executive said, "we made what was for us a startling discovery, which played a major role in our upsurge. We asked ourselves, 'what are the dimensions of a problem that make it profitable for us to solve?'

"One thing is that it must be well within our capability. We must be strong in that area. Another thing is that we know how to make money doing it. That usually means that our manufacturing has found a way to keep costs low, or that our salespeople can hang on to a premium price.

"We've also found a third characteristic. The problems we find really profitable to solve are those that can make an important contribution to the customer's profit. That means they cut the customer's costs significantly or they help him get new sales. If we can show him how that will happen, getting the price premium that gives us profit becomes easy."

"Everybody benefits," said another executive. "We don't squawk about the cost, the customer doesn't squawk about the price. But we can both crow about the values that are being added to the customer's business.

"There's even an additional value we've discovered. We've had an educational influence on our customers by our insistence on solving only profitable problems. As a result, they've been putting priorities on their own problems. Those that will be most profitable for them to solve go to the top. Those whose cost exceeds their value go out the window. I really get a kick out of hearing a customer say to me, 'You taught us something.' That helps solve one of my own problems—feeling I've served a man as well as sold him."

FIGURE 4.2
QUESTIONS TO PREVENT PROBLEMS

Situation	Actions
A key employee announces plans for retirement.	• Who is available on staff right now as a possible replacement?
	• How long will it take to train a replacement adequately to handle the retiree's job efficiently?
	• What ancillary problems can this retirement cause? (Liaison with other departments or individuals within the organization; effects on long-term customer relationships; possible decline in morale because others must pick up the slack until a replacement is on stream.)
	• What costs may be involved because of this retirement, and how are they to be resolved?
You've just signed a contract with a new supplier for your company.	• What other people and/or departments should be informed, and in what detail?
	• What new internal communication procedures will be required, as well as those with the new supplier?
	• What contracts must be developed between you and others within the company, and with suppliers?

Think Ahead

Not every problem is a matter of immediacy. Frequently looking ahead can identify those you will need to be concerned about in the future. Equally important, forward thinking can often save you time, money, and energy.

FIGURE 4.2 (continued)

Situation	Actions
A number of new employees will be brought on board within the next twelve to eighteen months.	• Has Human Resources been told the number needed, education required, experience demanded, etc.?
	• Have ads been prepared for insertion in appropriate media?
	• Has the training department been contacted, so it can gear up in time?
	• Have the various department heads been seen for their input concern- the new hires?
	• Have the necessary funds been appropriated?
Your child announces she plans to attend graduate school a year hence.	• What's this going to cost, and what sources of revenue can be tapped to secure the necessary funds?
	• Is it possible to obtain the degree at a local college or university? How cost-effective will this be? Will the degree carry the same prestige as that of an out-of-town or state institution?
	• In view of your youngster's future plans, how important will a graduate degree be to the chosen career?
	• How much additional time will be involved before your child is independent?

Figure 4.2 shows several typical situations in which the anticipation of problems can help to bring them under control, even before they occur.

In order to handle a problem well, you must try to anticipate the consequences. First, focus on the *analysis step* of the problem-solving procedure, then determine:

- What present circumstances suggest possible difficulties in the future?

- Who or what exactly is involved? Who else should be informed?

- How can the situation be averted—or converted—into an opportunity?

- When should a timetable or schedule of activities be prepared to bring the problem under control?

- Where can time and/or funds be found with which to fight the problem? How much of each will be required?

- When and under what circumstances must the best solution be ready for implementation?

Figure 4.3 (page 122) provides you with an opportunity to put the problem-solving formula we've discussed to work in a very practical way. While the forms themselves offer no solutions, they help bring problems into focus. The forms remind you of key areas to analyze, of facts and information to carefully check, and of factors to evaluate in terms of their importance. They help you make certain there will be no serious oversights—or rash judgments. Use Figure 4.3 to:

- *Define a problem* that is inhibiting progress in your life, on the job, or with others. Be sure to analyze any causes to define your problem more accurately and concisely.

- *Secure information* essential for bringing the problem into perspective.

- *In reaching a solution,* be sure you weigh and decide all factors involved.

- *Test possible alternatives* in determining a final solution.

- Be sure you *check results.*

Problem Solver's Profile

The most common characteristics of successful problem solvers are:

- The ability to remain cool under fire.

- A high degree of common sense.

- The willingness to hear others out without interruption.

- The courage to take action, however personally painful the solution may be.

- The tenacity to survive—pick up the pieces, repair what is spoiled, and start over!

Additionally, successful problem solvers have a knack for:

- Exuding a combination of personal confidence, assurance, and impatience. They're likely to be bluntly abrupt with those who remain indecisive.

- Looking positively at a problem situation. The

FIGURE 4.3

PROBLEM SOLVING WORKSHEET

1. When, who, and how was the problem first brought to your attention?

2. What was violated by this deviation from established standards?

3. Write out a brief statement of the problem, explaining:
   - What exactly is the present *unsatisfactory* level?
   - What would be *acceptable* performance?
   - How is this acceptable level of performance *determined*?
   - What are possible *causes* contributing to this unsatisfactory level?
   - List the most *likely* of these causes.

4. List possible solutions or proposed courses of action you feel will alleviate the situation.
   - There are three basic criteria to consider: *Practicality*—will the solution achieve the desired results? *Costs*—this includes not only dollars but time, and whether other people are involved. *Feasibility*—is it likely to happen? Is it worth the effort? What are its chances of working?
   - What impact will the various solutions have on morale?

5. Rate each solution in terms of its being high (H), medium (M), or low (L). Ideally the best solution is one that rates high in *practicality*, low as it concerns *costs*, and high as far as *feasibility* is concerned.

Solution Possibilities	Criteria for Rating								
	(✓) Practicality			(✓) Costs			(✓) Feasibility		
	H	M	L	H	M	L	H	M	L

6. Note the solution or solutions recommended that come closest to the "ideal" (high practicality, low cost, high feasibility).

7. Jot down an action plan, including the steps to be taken in sequence, for each of the best solutions. Be sure to indicate the follow up necessary to keep each solution on target.

risks involved in solving a problem, inconvenience, or costs do not receive much of their attention. Their attitude is more likely to be "Let's get on with it!"

- Quickly bringing problems under control, not just because it is their responsibility to do so, but because of their desire to excel and be recognized as achievers.

- Evaluating problems in terms of their effects rather than what others see as the side issues.

Blind But Never Bound

When friends first told us about Bob and Jennie Mahoney, I couldn't believe what I heard. Then, after reading the details of their story and talking to them, I was even more amazed. I vowed I would do my best to spread the inspirational message of their lives as far as possible.

The Mahoneys' blindness has never been a barrier to happiness or achieving their goals. Both blind since childhood, they raised ten children who grew up to be successful examples of their parents. Somehow, you have the strong feeling that **blindness made them unstoppable**. Page after page, I kept asking myself "If they can do all these things without seeing anything, anytime, what can I possibly complain about?" The truth is, they have been **blind but never bound**.

Bob served as representative to the Michigan state legislature for eighteen years. He always voted his principles with good conscience and was eventually defeated because of his unpopular stand on a very emotional issue—school busing.

In the early years of their marriage, Bob supported his rapidly growing family as a door-to-door salesman with his leader dog. Forty years ago, Bob and Jennie started their mail order business, Michigan Notary Service, which they still operate today.

The Mahoneys' cannot see the world as you and I can see it, yet they have insight—the ability to see **inside** themselves and **inside** others. With it they have overcome challenges that very few sighted people could handle.

Even more astounding is the fact that, as they struggled through what everyone but them would consider to be hardship, they held to their bedrock beliefs and commitments.

- They never expected results without effort.

- They did not ask for welfare or government assistance.

- They were always accountable for their own actions.

- They sought mutual benefit in all their relationships.

- They lived within their means.

- They combined hope with hard work.

- They constantly experimented with new ways to solve their problems.

- They changed before they had to.

- They lived their religious convictions.

Exemplary parents, successful entrepreneurs, tireless workers, perpetual risk takers, committed social activists who are brimming with good humor—the Mahoneys are one of the twentieth century's best examples of overcoming severe physical restrictions and adversity by putting personal values, moral convictions, and Christian faith into practice every day.

In Conclusion...How to Learn From Your Mistakes

- Take yourself aside for awhile everyday to think, to contemplate, to analyze, and to dream. Without mental exercise, we tend to repeat our mistakes.

- Always look for what's wrong before who's wrong. Don't get caught in the trap of always seeking someone to blame, including yourself. Find out what's wrong and fix it!

- Learn to be swayed more by facts than opinions. Give reasons for your conclusions and ask others to do the same.

- Become a problem solver. Keep in mind that problem bringers find more problems; problem solvers find solutions.

- Don't try to eliminate opposition. Use it to clarify your thinking and strengthen your position.

- Beware of competence without accomplishment. Even the best intentions have no value without results. Competent people who don't achieve are underemployed or mismatched.

- Remember, capability without achievement is wasteful.

Chapter 5

COPING WITH CONFLICT

Using Stress to Your Advantage

E MOTIONAL STRESS, MANY AUTHORITIES BELIEVE, CAN cause coronary artery disease. This disease has many roots, but more and more evidence is pointing to chronic emotional stress as a key factor. A person who works too hard, relaxes too little, and is always tense can experience changes that affect the arteries nourishing the heart. Historically an ailment of men, women—particularly women executives—are catching up. The stresses and conflicts we experience have found their way into our everyday language. How many times have you heard comments such as:

"It's a jungle out there!"

"Well...it's back to the old rat race."

"That's Jim for you! Always spinning his wheels."

"Life in this house is like a pressure cooker."

These comments suggest "downers" that are all too typical—satisfaction is either borderline or on the decline; conditions that could make our lives interesting and rewarding are just not there! The experts are telling us—in newspapers and magazines as well as a rash of new books—to avoid stress as we would the plague. They detail, with grim statistics, what stress can do to people. The facts are shocking:

- Twenty million Americans suffer from hypertension.

- One out of every ten persons drinks too much.

- Over one-third of all deaths are due to heart attacks; another ten percent result from strokes.

- One out of every three workers calls in sick daily because of some stress-related problem.

- One out of eight suicide attempts is fatal.

The list could go on and on. But, is stress such a real and personal danger? Maybe not.

Stress Is a Natural Function

Avoiding stress is as futile as shunning food or love or exercise. Stress is as normal a function of the body as breathing and a heartbeat. It is the body's reaction to an emotion, whether real or imagined.

The major fact about stress is that *it cannot be*

avoided. Equally important, it is essential to our well-being. Without this built-in stress mechanism, few of us would live very long. There would be no way of mobilizing the body's defenses to reduce physical or emotional damage.

We are bombarded constantly throughout our lives by stressful situations. Each can affect our behavior with friends, with family, or on the job. We must understand that, at its best, stress primes us for peak performance. It stimulates and increases our energy levels. It can, for some people, improve vision and even sharpen their thinking.

At its worst, stress can interfere with our ability to think and act normally. If stretched to the breaking point, it will cause a breakdown. No matter how tough or resilient we think we may be, each of us has a breaking point that can render us helpless.

Those who might strive for a life utterly free of stress would probably be disappointed with the results. Chances are one of two things might occur: either they would live the life of a vegetable, or in trying to avoid external stress, they would create their own form of internal stress.

Stress does not always appear suddenly or as the result of some especially traumatic event. Frustration over time, because it is constant and irritating, can bring unrelenting anxiety and feelings of inadequacy.

Fortunately, most of the time we develop resistance

to the stress we encounter. As we learn to master stressful conditions, our anxieties tend to dissipate. The next time they occur, less stress is experienced. Over time, we can raise our resistance to it.

What Do You Mean By Stress?

Stress is the body's physical and mental response to what the mind perceives as exciting, challenging, confusing, or dangerous. Stress is in the person; stressors, the cause of stress, are in the environment. Typically stressors include such things as heat, cold, certain other people, objects, events or situations that cause alarm. They place a physical or psychological demand on us that affects our equilibrium.

Stress is our response to a stressor. Each of us reacts differently to situations depending on circumstances, experience, and/or inherited traits. Stress is:

- **Inescapable.** It is a part of every human's experience. Some people actively seek out stressful situations: sky divers, soldiers of fortune, and race car drivers.

- **Personal.** No two people are affected in the same way by an identical stressor. Some can brush it off as inconsequential. It may cause others to climb the walls—and what failed to faze a person in the morning may prove to be a disastrous situation only a few hours later. While tolerance to stress will differ from person to person, one fact stands out: **those who take poor care of their physical needs are more likely to be overwhelmed by stress.**

- **Cumulative.** Though not a perpetual motion machine, stress, once started, has a tendency to feed on itself.

- **A behavioral influence.** Positive stresses generate benefits. Negative stresses can cause worries, doubts, and even physical disorders. They can actually interfere with the solution to a problem.

- **An asset or a liability.** Properly managed, stress can be a powerful motivator. If too intense, however, it can create both physical and mental damage.

- **Physical.** Stress is intended to enable a physical response to a physical threat, whether actual or perceived.

These are some of the characteristics common to stress. But what actually happens when you learn your mother-in-law plans to spend the next three months with the family, your boss calls you in for a little chat, the bank telephones about two checks that have bounced, your daughter at college calls home to announce she thinks she may be pregnant, or your brother-in-law asks for a big loan?

You know the feeling. You break into a sweat. You tremble. You may describe the sensation as being "uptight." If you'll recall some of the circumstances in which stress plays a leading role, four related processes come to mind.

1. Your body mobilizes itself instantly to take action.

2. There is a sharp increase in energy consumption. The body becomes sensitized, alert, ready to respond to the stressor, to run or to fight, as the case may be.

3. The muscular action involved in the fight or flight response is experienced. Here's where the action takes place—you either slug it out with the stressor or, depending on the circumstances, skip the valor and run.

4. Finally, when the stress response subsides, the body returns to normal.

These are the external reactions: what you feel and how you respond. They are the actions you take. But what goes on internally? How does the body get set viscerally?

When a stressful event is encountered, changes occur rapidly all over the body. These changes are designed to protect you from physical harm or emotional damage. Emotional reactions are centered in that part of the brain called the hypothalamus, which controls the severity of the body's physical reaction to emotional stress and whose function is to recognize and evaluate stressors.

Once this is done it sends appropriate messages through a network of nerves to the pituitary gland, which responds to the brain's messages and triggers a rush of adrenaline from the adrenal glands. These glands produce hormones that regulate blood pressure and the supply of energy. They stimulate heart and blood pressure, muscles, and lungs to improve blood flow, oxygen consumption and strength. The liver, spleen, digestive system, and other organs are also activated.

How does all this work in real life? Take the case of a boxer sweating out a bout. Even before he climbs into the ring his body readies itself. Defenses against physical damage are mobilized. The brain is transmitting split-second messages to various muscles telling some to relax and others to tense up for action.

The identical phenomena hold true for the youngsters about to visit the principal's office for some rule infraction, except that in this instance the body prepares itself against emotional injury.

At the end of the bout or discussion with the principal, the brain's stress messages subside and body functions return to normal. Without these reactions, however, the fighter and the youngster might have been in deep trouble. Fortunately, both were keyed up, and therefore strengthened and better able to take on the situations in which they were involved. Stress saved the day.

Coaches make positive use of stress in training their athletes. The main qualities successful coaches seek in an athlete are self-confidence, competitiveness, and the ability to accept and learn from defeat. Obviously these qualities don't occur in a single day. They develop because of a well-organized program. The skills an athlete learns are transferable to whatever he or she might want to do in life.

Concerning stress, the coach feels athletes do well—when they want to do well—regardless of an event's importance. Simply performing well to please the crowd does not make for top performance, only more pressure is added. Positive thinking occurs when an athlete says, "I want to perform well, because that's what I want to do. That's my goal. Now what do I have to do to achieve it?"

What About Chronic Stress?

Chronic stress is a different story. Unless brought under control within a reasonable length of time, the damage it can cause is enormous. Physicians are convinced it is responsible for such diseases as ulcers, asthma, high blood pressure, arthritis, and overactive thyroid glands—among other physical problems.

It has been discovered that psychosomatic diseases occur when people are psychologically stressed. When exposed to psychological stress, one is likely to react with a particular emotion. Should this emotion affect one part of the body more than others, an organ can become vulnerable. The longer the stress continues, the greater the chance the organ will eventually become diseased.

It isn't hard to imagine the damage rejection might do to the physical and emotional well-being of men and women in sales. Unless they can take turndowns in stride, the constant repetition of no can easily erode their confidence and their health.

Ed McMahon, recognized as one of television's top stars, discovered at an early age that he had an ability to sell. He also quickly discovered that rejection is as much a part of selling as are customers to be sold. How does this pro handle such situations? The biggest challenge he believes is to learn how to take the sting out of rejection. This is because being rejected isn't something we invented. It doesn't happen to us alone. It's possible to secure a huge success, then experience a series of depressing failures. Men and women who sell for a living know they're going to be turned down. That's the nature of the work—it comes with the territory. **You can't be a salesperson without failing.** Everyone must find a way to overcome it. You must have confidence to know that sooner or later you'll get back on target. McMahon vividly remembers being fired once without even knowing why. He found out that it was because a producer had objected to a joke he told on the air. That same producer, however, asked

him several years later to host two shows for him.
Moral: hang in there!

> I've never known a person who was lucky for
> a long time. They all deserved what they had.
> For example, there is no such thing as a lucky
> marathon runner.

Experts are in universal agreement that rejection is
actually the fodder for acceptance and achievement.
Jesse Owens, the hero of the 1936 Olympic Games in
Berlin, felt as rejected as any human possibly could.
Born the son of a sharecropper, and sickly most of his
childhood, few believed he would ever be athletic
enough to compete in a sport. As he matured, however,
Owens became convinced that rejection was actually
correction.

What he meant is that when someone is rejected,
the person doing the turning down is either correct—or
incorrect.

If correct, something of significance will have been
learned. Something that will help win the next time
around. Even if that person is incorrect, something
valuable will result from the turndown. That person
will learn that the world isn't always right in its rejec-
tions, and in the end, it may have to pay for its mistake.

Stress is also the result of facing the unknown consequences of change. It is directly related to the degree

of change required for the adoption of new ways of doing things. It grows increasingly intense as a person moves from a call to alter usual practices and procedures to changes in values, orientation, and basic motives.

A change of any kind results in stress, because it challenges a person's sense of adequacy.

That's what usually happens to employees when a business changes hands, particularly in these days of fast-moving mergers and acquisitions. Stress becomes an ever-present fact of life for many who once felt secure in their jobs, who enjoyed their authority, and felt confident about the future. But the day a firm is acquired by another, employees—from executives to middle managers to clerical workers—are likely to feel the strain.

By losing independence, management at nearly every acquired company also loses stature. Executives used to calling the shots start reporting to a layer of management above them. And a number inevitably are dismissed because the parent company doesn't need two people for every corporate slot.

If this were not stressful enough, consider the signals from new bosses that indicate changes are clearly in order. Criticism of past management practices and results is not likely to calm jittery nerves. Many will be told to move on, others will be asked to retire, and some will simply quit to avoid being fired. Others can anticipate demotion, or a sharp curtailment of their authority.

The Causes of Stress

The causes for stress are everywhere—at home, on the job, with friends, and in the environment. If these are not enough, consider age as an example. Each age experiences stressors peculiar to that group, ranging from total dependence in infancy, to the meanderings of adolescence, to the pressures unique to adult life. No doubt about it, we live stressful lives.

As we grow older, the physical and emotional changes experienced are cause for stress. The same holds true for changes taking place on the job. They can range from a confrontation with the boss to technologies that can eliminate an occupation completely.

> I love to watch other people out on the golf course. For instance, you can always spot an employee playing golf with his boss. He's the one who has a great shot and says, "Oooops!"

Stress in one area can cause stresses in others. A kid in trouble can cause dad's work to suffer on the job, which in turn generates stresses in other areas. Figure 5.1 lists examples of events most people consider stressful.

Psychologists agree that ranking jobs by the amount

of stress they induce is practically impossible because stress is highly individual. Still, attempts are made. The National Institute of Occupational Safety and Health examined admission records of community health centers in one state. The most stressful jobs, in descending order of stress, were as follows:

1. Health Technician
2. Waiter/Waitress
3. Practical Nurse
4. Inspector
5. Musician
6. Public Relations
7. Clinical Lab Tech
8. Dishwasher
9. Warehouseman
10. Nurse's Aid
11. Laborer
12. Dental Assistant
13. Teacher's Aid
14. Research Worker
15. Computer Programmer
16. Photographer
17. Telephone Operator
18. Hairdresser
19. Painter/Sculptor
20. Health Aid
21. Taxi Driver
22. Chemist

FIGURE 5.1
STRESSFUL SITUATIONS

Stressors at Home	On the Job	In Society
Death of a spouse	Fired	Breaking the law
Divorce	Retirement	Changes in political structure
Marital separation	Promotion	Change in friends
Death of family member	Demotion	Inflation
Personal injury or illness	Business readjustment	Social mores change
Marriage	Job with new company	Disasters
Marital reconciliation	Responsibility changes	New dress habits
Change in health of family member	Outstanding achievement	Money (plus or minus)
Pregnancy	Work hour changes	
Sexual problems	Changes in conditions of work	
New family member	Competition	
Change in financial state	Performance review	
Death of close friend or family member	Changes in performance standards	
Change in residence	Money (plus or minus)	
Change in sleeping habits		
Change in eating habits		
Vacation		
Christmas		
Children leave home		
Arguments in the home		
Money (plus or minus)		

In the "real" world, stress affects assembly line work-ers who contend they never have time for a drink of water or for talking; and that their job is not only fast and hard, but boring. Their minds want to wander, but they have to keep concentrating, even though the noise drives them to move faster and faster to the point of mental collapse.

Business executives may work fifty to sixty hours a week, with heads of companies putting in as much as ten to twenty hours more. The job is more important than anything else in their lives—including friends, recreation, and even family! They stay late at the office, then take work home with them at night. Weekends are used for business rather than getting reacquainted with the family. What's more, the pace is faster now than ever before—so fast that executives these days are seldom free to entertain new ideas or innovative approaches.

Even people with open-ended jobs typically feel frus-trated by an inability to complete everything they plan.

On the positive side, those who love their jobs face the constant agony of making choices between highly-desirable alternatives. They spend lots of time regret-ting that their days do not have double the hours in which to do more of the things they find exciting, prof-itable, and worthwhile.

Figure 5.2 presents a summary of stresses and stres-sors.

FIGURE 5.2
STRESS/STRESSOR SUMMARY

Definition:
- Any action or situation that places a psychological or physical demand on a person. Something that unbalances one's equilibrium, whether real or imagined.

Types:
- Internal stressors are those put on oneself.
- External stressors stem from family, friends, or the environment.

Characteristics:
- Tangible/intangible.
- Situations that seem threatening, burdensome, or likely to cause stress.
- Heat, cold, noise, chemicals, etc.
- Emotional difficulties.
- Work or interpersonal relationships.

Typical Stress Situations:
- Driving
- Loneliness
- Criticism
- Deadlines

Stress Categories:
- Physical (heat/cold)
- Time
- Emotional (fears/tears)
- Unpredictable events
- Anxiety about what will happen next
- Too many alternatives
- Discrimination, manipulation, demeaning behavior

Facts to Remember:
- Stressors are anything that block the satisfaction of human needs.
- Changes, especially when swift, generate stress.
- Events over which one has no control or that represent loss of a thing of value are most stressful.
- Anything that happens for the first time, or that cannot be made sense of immediately, will trigger stress.
- The key to success is in identifying stressors in your life and learning how to manage them before they get out of hand and endanger health.

Coping With Stress

Most of us can handle everyday headaches with relative ease. We've faced them before, and refuse to be hassled by the small stuff. Some people can even shrug off intense pressures and get on with what they have to do. They keep their perspective and refuse to choke-up over things they can't change, while others react violently to even trivial things.

Stress affects us on both a physical and emotional level; so we must learn to cope with it. No one is immune. Premature death from hypertension threatens women as much as it does men. Mothers trying to be everything to everyone all at the same time are at risk. So are career woman who can afford help at home, but do not have it. A recent survey revealed that among persons with MBAs, four times more women than men suffered from stress.

Figure 5.3 provides practical suggestions to keep stress under control.

Handling the Stressful Situation

> The men and women who win have been counted out many times. They just didn't bother listening to the referee.

As we have seen, stress may result from fatigue or overwork; some threat to our security, self-esteem, or basic

FIGURE 5.3
CONTROLLING STRESS

PHYSICAL FACTORS

- Tense people tend to hold their breath, which only increases tension. Concentrate on deep, steady breathing.

- Smoking, drinking, popping pills, poor eating habits, and insufficient sleep all contribute to stress. The better shape you're in, the better you can handle anything that comes along.

- Seek variety. Stay out of ruts. Find something that has a pace that's different, goals that are different from those you pursue regularly. Try a new hobby or sport.

- Under stress there's a tendency to withdraw from others. Instead, draw strength from the people close to you.

- You do yourself no favors by avoiding medical care when ill. Seek aid promptly to prevent damage to your body, and to reduce the vulnerability of that part of your body to stress.

EMOTIONAL FACTORS

- Accept stress as a challenge to know yourself better, so that you can develop your own potential. Determine the activities or responsibilities you aim to avoid.

- Watch how you react to negative situations. Ask yourself, "Which is more important to me, to achieve something significant or to avoid failure?" Then resolve to handle failure as you pursue *significant* performance.

- Pinpoint your own level of stress. Determine the point at which you're affected by it and prepare for it.

- Decide how to eliminate obstacles that smother growth. Refuse to cope with an obstacle you can remove.

- List the conflicts that disturb you, and take steps to resolve them. This will help you grow.

- Failure alone shouldn't keep you awake at night. It is the rejection experienced in a failure that creates concern. Make it a major personal goal to condition yourself so you can cope with rejection.

- Don't think of failure only as a learning experience, but also as an opportunity to try something new.

- Be careful to make life-style changes in small steps. Every time you have a small success—celebrate!

- Understand that failure and success are both part of the same process of achieving. In effect, one must know how to feel successful even though you may fall short of your goal.

- Try to accentuate the positive. Doing so will give you a better chance to avoid becoming a grump.

- **Expect conflict and stress!**

goals in living; adjustments to new experiences; or rapidly changing environmental factors.

While there are no guaranteed techniques to eliminate stress, a number of common sense guides are very helpful.

- State the problem to a confidant. This tends to broaden perspectives and unclutter the mind, so it possible to arrive at a sensible course of action. Select someone you can trust, who is not only an excellent listener but who can keep your confidence.

- Relax. Don't sweat the small stuff—that's what life is mostly about. Not only will you live longer, but you will solve problems faster and with better results.

- Fight or flee. There are no medals to be won in fighting a rear-guard action just to keep fighting. If a situation has no chance for improvement (a lousy job you hate or a hopeless relationship) stress can be reduced dramatically by making a change.

- Do something. If the stress is strong enough to bother you, take action. Chances are it won't get better if you wait. Actually, if you procrastinate, you are likely to suffer even more emotionally and physically.

- Exercise control. Put yourself in position to either

blunt or halt the stress that's causing the conflict or pressure. If loud noises distract you at home, shut the door. If you must make an important presentation, prepare. If you have something to get off your chest, say it as tactfully as you can.

- Pat yourself on the back. When you've been eyeball to eyeball with a stressful event and successfully faced it down—congratulate yourself. Not only has your skill brought it under control, but you can now take on other stressors with greater confidence.

Successful people bounce back from stress because of their positive attitude. No matter how bleak things look, they maintain an optimistic inner spirit that helps them surmount obstacles. To them defeat is merely a temporary setback.

Dunce or Genius?

Paul Orfalea (or-fa-la) is the founder and chairman of Kinkos, the twenty-four-hour copy and printing chain. His curly red hair got him the nickname kinko. With a personal worth over a quarter of a billion dollars, he likes to tell people that he came out of school unemployable. At age forty-nine, he now knows that all through his school years, his dyslexia went undiagnosed and untreated. Result? He could barely read or write. A misfit in school, he learned business fundamentals from his Lebanese parents' store in the Los Angeles garment district. From a copy shop he ran as a college student near Santa Barbara in 1970, he has built Kinkos to 860 stores. The goal is to have 2,000 by the year 2,000 and a global network soon thereafter. The company even has its own on-line service called Kinkonet.

His favorite pastime is interviewing customers, but he also likes to get the employees' perspective by working behind the counter making copies or sweeping floors. Every year, Orfalea and members of the Board of Directors take the place of employees in the store with the highest profitability.

His financial partners call him a business genius and an idea-generating machine—not bad for a kid placed in a class for the mentally slow in grade school!

One of the primary aims of this book is to help you help yourself; not just with advice and guidelines, but with down-to-earth, practical ideas, that will help you bring chronic stress under control. That's the purpose of the exercise in Figure 5.4.

As an initial step, you'll find it helpful to identify and list your worst stressors. If you're stuck for a moment, refer to Figure 5.1 for some thought-starters. Do not limit yourself to this list, however. Address stressors that affect you personally, are causing conflict at home or on the job, that put you under heavy pressure, and that to date *defy successful solution.*

FIGURE 5.4

EFFECTS OF YOUR STRESSORS

Indicate the frequency with which the stressors you've listed occur, including their severity and their effect on you as well as others.			
Stressor	Frequency	Severity	Effect

What have you done to cope with or eliminate these stressors?

Why do you feel they still persist?

Jot down how you plan to bring the stressors and stresses they spawn under control. Review the section titled "Handling the Stressful Situation" for ideas and suggestions. Then develop a plan of action.

What is the **most important** stressor you want to eliminate first?	How long do you estimate it will take to bring this stressor under control?

FIGURE 5.4 (continued)

Why is it important this particular one be eliminated before the others?	Are there any **costs** involved (time, money, other people?)
How was this stressor brought to your attention?	What **benefits** will accrue to you (and others) when this stress/stressor has been eliminated?
What **resources** or **assistance** will be needed?	How has this stressor generated stresses in other areas of your life?

The Steps to Solution	
What will be your **first step**?	
List the **subsequent steps** in the order you will take them.	
How will you **check** to be certain the stressor is no longer a cause of stress to you?	

When the stress caused by this stressor has been eliminated or brought under control, take on the others you have listed in the order of their priority to you, your family, and your associates. Follow the same format in your planning.

> Great occasions don't make heroes or cowards. They simply unveil them to the eyes of others. Silently and imperceptibly, as we wake or sleep, we grow and get stronger, or we grow and get weaker. Then, at last, some crisis shows us what we have become.

In Conclusion...Overcoming Opposition

- Identify areas in which friends, associates, family, or spouse need help the most. Then become an expert in as many of these areas as possible.

- When you've expressed an opinion and have listened attentively to the opposition, excuse yourself for a few minutes to consider, in private, the various options open to you.

- If you must disagree, don't be disagreeable.

- Following a serious clash of opinions, take time to calmly write down your opponent's key points as concisely as possible. Under each point, jot down at least one benefit to those who oppose your views if they accept your proposition. Be sure to decide which of their points you can accept and which ones you must reject. Present your analysis along with its benefits the next time you meet.

- Whenever you win an argument, make certain your opponent can retire gracefully without loss of face. Your objective is progress, not destruction. Who knows what allies you may need in the future? Besides, you can never totally destroy an idea.

- If you don't want others to succeed, forget about being a leader.

Chapter 6

ARE YOU UNSTOPPABLE?

WE HAVE A CHOICE IN LIFE. WE CAN LEARN TO GIVE IN, or become unstoppable. This is what we learn from unstoppable people:

1. **Never allow fear to prevent you from trying.**

    Bill Gates is the richest American ever ($38 billion at last count) because he continues to venture into new computer-related technologies... even when some of them fail resoundingly.

2. **Realize that only you control what you can become.**

    Sam Walton ignored those who urged him to put profit before people. He built the largest retail chain in the world in less than ten years. He did it so silently, Sears never heard him coming.

3. **Tolerate pain and you will hurt less.**

> **Christopher Reeves,** although paralyzed below the neck, refuses to believe he is helpless and continues an active life as an outstanding actor and director.

> **Helen Keller** was deaf, blind and speechless, yet she found ways to communicate with and inspire everyone who learned of her work.

> **Gwen Frostic** was spastic from birth, and barely able to walk or speak. She has thrilled millions for decades with her inspired drawings and poetry focusing on nature's beauty, bounty, and mysteries. She is now ninety-two.

4. **Listen to those who love you.**

> **Dewitt Wallace,** after military service in World War I, accepted the challenge of his minister father's life savings as a loan and the total commitment of his young wife to start what would become the largest circulation magazine of all time—*The Readers Digest.*

5. **Accept that your only accomplishments are what you have overcome.**

> **Sandra Day O'Connor,** after raising her family and a low profile career in the judicial system, became the first woman to serve on the U.S.

Supreme Court. She is now acknowledged as the most influential member of that body.

6. **Acknowledge gifts as the opposite of achievements.**

    Mohandas K. Gandhi personified passive resistance to oppression, temperance, self-sacrifice, and empathetic wisdom. Many believe he was surpassed in these attributes only by Jesus Christ. His lifelong work opened the gates to India's freedom.

7. **Change before you must.**

    Howard Hughes innherited millions, and acquired many more, but became so self-centered, paranoid, insecure, and deranged that he died sick, diseased, despised, miserable, and alone.

8. **Believe tomorrow will be better.**

    Oprah Winfrey was born in poverty and raised by her grandmother, but she refused to look backward as she built the largest TV production company controlled by an individual. Her net worth is well over $500 million.

9. **Get up one more time.**

    Vince Lombardi converted football losers to winners with a simple creed: "Football

games are won by players who do two
things. First, they knock their opponent
down, then they get up again!"

10. **Understand that admiration and wealth are fleeting.**

> **Andrew Carnegie** came to the U.S. as a penniless boy from Scotland. His wealth in today's dollars is estimated at $42 billion. To express appreciation for his good fortune, he gave away millions to build scores of libraries, museums, and cultural centers. But, to be certain his outlook would be remembered accurately, Carnegie wrote his own epitaph. It reads: "Here lies a man who enlisted in his service better men than himself."

I rest my case.

Chapter 7

PUTTING IT ALL TOGETHER

WHERE DO YOU GO FROM HERE? YOU HAVE FOCUSED on areas of prime importance to your success in life. More importantly, you now have an opportunity to tailor the ideas and approaches suggested in this book so that they conform to the reality you face in your daily contacts. The methods *will* work.

There is, however, one more essential step for you to handle. Success will depend on your willingness to take action and *get the important things done in your life!* Only then will you really define your values, develop self-confidence, convert problems into opportunities, rise above conflict—and make the time you've invested up to this point pay off.

Action is essential to achieving success. Skill in analyzing problems and identifying opportunities is important, of course. But it is impossible to pinpoint an opportunity or solve a problem *without actually doing it.*

Part of this doing rests upon knowing when to end analysis and get on with what must be done. Often it becomes more important to select a course of action than to continue a debate in the hope of choosing the absolute best.

Another part of doing involves frequent review of the material in this book, and applying the principles and techniques to the decisions you must make. Not only will this keep you apprised of the conditions you encounter, it will increase your self-confidence because you will know what steps to take.

I am a third-generation American. My great-grandparents on both sides came to the United States in the 1860s and 1890s from Germany, Norway, and Holland. Now in my late sixties, I have been looking back more than ever before. I find myself wondering what difference it makes when and where you are born. This is where my thoughts have led.

My dad was a high school dropout. Most of the time he held two jobs, working evenings and weekends. He walked to work or rode a bike. When a majority of the people beside him held college degrees, his answer was simple—he'd do the things they didn't want to do and he'd do them better. He didn't make excuses; he didn't even pause for regrets; he just kept going. His legacy to me: "Just do it!"

My maternal grandfather was the son of Norwegian immigrants who came to America as indentured servants. He lived ninety-four years and ten months. Most of that time he did hard physical work. With less than five years of schooling, he died owning two farms and having earned the respect of everyone who knew him.

My wife's father became head of the household at age fourteen when his father was killed in a farming accident. Although he was not the oldest son, he took charge; supported his mother and saw that his brothers and sister received a college education. With a fierce independence and commitment to honesty, hard work, and no shortcuts, his heritage was to remove the fear of failure from the lives of his own four children.

As a child, my wife developed problems in expressing herself. When we met at age nineteen, she was very shy. But behind the scenes and beneath the surface I found her to be a human dynamo. She can outwork anyone I have ever known,. In the process of deciding she would not be inferior, she has developed skills few others can match. But mostly, she cares—about me, our daughters, her family, her friends, elderly neighbors, and shut-ins. Like her mother, she is wearing herself out helping others. I can see the toll—the age in her eyes; the stooping shoulders; the exhaustion at day's end. But my words can't stop her and I must quit trying.

No one can tell her what she must do or must not do. She knows what she wants—she wants to help—and she will!

Our two daughters are what sociologists would call "children of affluence." Within reason, they have had whatever money could buy—clothes, cars, vacations, college. They have traveled extensively in this country and abroad. Yet they have both grown to be conscientious, responsible adults. They are creative, persistent, mature young women who prefer to be accountable for their actions and are rising in their chosen professions of management and teaching. We are very proud of them.

One night, when I was fifteen, I was awakened by an excruciating pain in my lower back. What I thought was a football injury turned out to be polio. For fifty-five years I have told myself, "If you let this slow you down, any other excuse will also." I am proud that I didn't quit.

I am grateful to my parents for challenging me. I am better off because no one told me they would take care of me. In my college days, I worked summers full-time on road-paving crews, and part-time in several jobs the rest of the year, to earn $1,500 to pay all of my college expenses. Now, it is not unusual for me to make several times that amount in one day.

There is a common thread in these examples. It is not ambition or luck or destiny. It is opportunity! What is its source? That's the best part of all. It comes as a gift, a gift from God. God decides where and when we will be born, and for a very privileged minority (only two-and-a-half percent of the world's population) it comes from the people of the United States of America. It is because the people of our country continue to believe in opportunity that they are able to keep it alive and thriving for people like me and millions yet to come. Thank God for America—thank America for opportunity.

In everyday life, we are all exposed to prejudice, tangled emotions, and even outright stupidity. The idea is not to ignore them or to find a cure for them, but to overcome them. Your most important asset in doing this is you-but only if you start now to get that One Step Ahead! Here's to you!

BIBLIOGRAPHY

American Way magazine, November 1997

Executive Excellence magazine, March 1997

Fritz, Roger, *How to Manage Your Boss*, Career Press, 1994

Fritz, Roger, *Personal Performance Contracts*, Crisp Publications, 3rd Edition, 1993

Fritz, Roger, *The Entrepreneurial Family*, McGraw Hill, 1992

Fritz, Roger, *You're In Charge*, Scott, Foresman & Company, 1986

Lessons In Leadership magazine, February 1997

Mahoney, Robert, *Living Out of Sight*, 1995

Personal Excellence magazine, November 1997

Remsberg, Bonnie, *Success* magazine, January 1982

Strauss, William and Howe, Neil, *The Fourth Turning: An American Prophesy*, Broadway Books, Division of Bantam, Doubleday, Dell

ABOUT THE AUTHOR

D R. ROGER FRITZ WRITES AND SPEAKS FROM FORTY years' experience as an educator, manager, corporate executive, university president, and highly successful consultant to over 300 clients. President of Organization Development Consultants, he is respected throughout the country for his creative yet practical advice on how individuals and organizations can improve and grow. Many audiences benefit each year from the stimulating ideas in his live presentations. He serves four companies as a member of their board of directors.

Dr. Fritz is the author of thirty books, monthly columns in two national magazines, video programs, software, and thirty audio cassettes. His ideas have a daily influence on how Americans increase their effectiveness.

INDEX

ADDITIONAL INFORMATION

For more information about Dr. Roger Fritz's consulting and presentation topics or for information regarding books, audio tapes, CD-ROMs, reprints, software and other products, contact:

Organization Development Consultants

Phone: 630.420.7673

Fax 630.420.7835

Email: RFritz3800@aol.com

Web site: http://www.rogerfritz.com